FACTFINDER GUIDE

HORSES

FACTFINDER GUIDE
HORSES

Edited by
Sarah Harris

PRC

This edition first published in 1999 by
PRC Publishing Ltd,
Kiln House, 210 New Kings Road, London SW6 4NZ

ISBN 1 85648 526 9

Printed and bound in China

Credits for Factfinder Guide: Horses

The publisher gratefully acknowledges the contribution of the following photographers and photographic libraries, who provided the illustrations for this book:

Animal Photography (Sally Anne Thompson) for pages 2(both), 3(left), 6-7, 8, 12, 13, 15, 16, 17(both), 18, 21, 24, 25, 26, 27, 28, 32, 33(both), 34, 35, 38, 39(both), 40, 41, 42(both), 46, 47, 48, 49, 53(top), 54(both), 55, 56, 57(both), 58, 59(both), 60, 61, 62, 63(both), 64, 65, 66, 68, 70, 71, 72, 73, 74, 75, 77, 78, 79, 80, 81, 82, 85, 86, 87, 88, 89, 90, 91, 92, 93(top), 94, 95, 102, 103, 104, 105(both), 107, 110, 111, 112, 113, 114, 115, 116, 117, 121, 122, 123, 127, 128, 129, 130, 131, 133(top), 136, 137, 138, 141(both), 142, 143(bottom), 145, 146, 147, 148, 151, 153;

Bob Langrish for pages 3(right), 20, 22, 37, 44, 45 (both), 76, 96, 98, 99, 100, 101(both), 108, 109(both), 125, 126, 133(bottom), 134, 135, 156, 157;

Animal Photography (R.T.Willbie) for pages 9, 11, 19, 23, 43, 53(bottom), 67, 69, 83, 93(bottom), 106, 118, 119;

Animal Photography (V.NikiForov) for pages 10, 29, 30-31, 140, 143(top), 158, 159;

Image Bank (Zhen Ge Peng) for page 14;

Only Horses for page 36, (Dusty L Perin) for pages 120, 124;

Image Bank (Cheng An Zhao) for page 51;

Kit Houghton for pages 97, 139.

CONTENTS

INTRODUCTION

HISTORY OF THE HORSE

Early Ancestors

Like all animals, the horse as we know it today has undergone vast evolutionary changes since its earliest forebears first walked the earth. Scientists have traced the origins of the modern horse back to the Eocene period, more than 50 million years ago. At this time there lived a creature called Eohippus, which is the horse's earliest known ancestor. No bigger than dogs, Eohippus fossils have been found across North America and also in Europe.

During the Eocene period, much of the earth was covered with damp, swampy ground, and, to give a firm footing on such a surface, the Eohippus was equipped with a padded foot and toes — four on the forefeet and three on the hind feet. The teeth of the Eohippus were very different too, being smaller and suitable for grinding the plant shoots that constituted its main diet.

However, over a period of time both the environment and climate of the earth changed and, in order to survive, animals had to be able to adapt to new conditions. By the Oligocene period, around 30 million years ago, the climate was considerably cooler, and the predominantly lush, moist landscape had dried considerably. This meant that the ground was much firmer, and there was less

ICELAND HORSES

CAMARGUE

need for the balancing, gripping toes. The descendant of the Eohippus, the Mesohippus, now walked on three toes, the middle of which was considerably larger than the others. The Mesohippus could no longer rely on new plant shoots at ground level for food, and increasingly needed to reach higher, mature plant growth. Consequently the animal was now larger in size than its Eohippus ancestor. Teeth too, had adapted to assist feeding on coarser, harder material.

The next stage in development came with the Merychippus, living a further ten million years later, in the Miocene era. Once again, the size of the animal, and consequently its body weight, had increased, and the central single toe was used the most, with the side toes almost useless at this point. As the Miocene era gave way to the Pliocene, so arrived the latest horse ancestor, called the Pliohippus. The relationship to the modern day horse is clearly apparent at this point. Its height, at around four feet was comparable to today's small breeds, and the Pliohippus walked on a single toe, or hoof. The second and third toes had by now completely disappeared.

Finally, around one and a half million years ago, the Equus caballus appeared. The single hoof was now fully developed, the teeth were larger and suitable for grinding and chewing a wide variety of foodstuffs, and the eyes were placed to the side of the head, rather than to the front as its forebears' had been. The proportions of the Equus were also different from its ancestors. It had much longer legs, giving it the speed and pace it needed to escape from predators. This then was the first animal that we could truly recognize as a horse today.

The Changing World

It is clear that horses had to adapt physically in order to survive the changes in the earth's climate and environment. However, these changes also forced the

KUSHUM

early horses, along with other types of animal, to make changes in their location. Fossil remains show that the earliest ancestors of the horse, the Eohippus, were populous in Europe and North America. At this period of the earth's history its climate would have been primarily tropical. However, as the earth's temperature cooled, so regions north of the equator also cooled, and many animals migrated to the warmer lands of the south, or perished. The most dramatic of these temperature changes occurred during the ice ages, and it is the last and greatest Ice Age that appears to have had the most devastating effect on the equine world. Through migration to avoid the cold, or simply through dying out, horses effectively disappeared from North America and probably from many European regions as well. Although it is possible that small groups of especially hardy horses may have survived, horses are believed to have been extinct in these areas until their reintroduction many centuries later.

Following the Ice Age, horses were found in only a few areas of the world, mainly in the warmer regions of Asia and the Middle East. These horses began to develop into distinct types, which depended on the climate and conditions of the environment they lived in. Three principal types are recognized today. These are the Asiatic Wild Horse, descendants of which still exist today, the Diluvian Horse, native of northern Europe, and the Tarpan, which was found in eastern Europe and parts of the former Soviet Union. It is generally believed today that all modern horse breeds can trace their ancestry back to one of these types.

Horses and Man

It would appear that horses first began to be domesticated around 5,000-6,000 years ago, making it one of the last animals to have been domesticated by humans. The dog was the first, around 12,000 years ago, with sheep following 1,000 years later, and cattle around 9,000 years ago. It is likely that this first occurred in the Far or Middle East, although it is not possible to be certain.

Domestication was not the first interaction between man and horse, however. For centuries before their taming, horses were a major food source for man, and were frequently hunted. A popular method of hunting horses was to stampede a herd, and by using spears and flaming torches to direct them, drive as many animals as possible over cliffs or into ravines.

It is not known how or why humans first decided to domesticate the wild horse. Certainly the fact that it took a comparatively long time to make the

CAMARGUE

attempt must depend in part upon the temperament of the wild horse. Their pride, aggression, and fierce independence, coupled with their not inconsiderable size, must have made the task of taming the horse somewhat formidable.

Initially, it is probable that horses were kept as herd animals, rather like sheep and cattle. These horses would have been valuable sources of meat, milk, and hides. Indeed, nomadic tribesmen in remote parts of the world still employ horses in this manner. From this beginning, the use of horses as pack animals, and later as riding mounts, must have been a natural progression.

For centuries the ownership of horses was regarded as an important gauge of wealth and horses were prized and cared for as valuable assets. This veneration can be seen in the large part horses have played in pre-Christian cultures. In Ancient Greece, the best horses were kept for ceremonial sacrifice and several Gods were depicted as traveling on horses. Paintings and carvings from places as distant as India, Europe, and China also show horses playing a central role in the daily life of societies.

The use of horses for transportation opened up the world to explorers and conquerors as never before. Long distances could be traveled in considerably less time, and equipment and supplies carried with ease. It was soon discovered

that traveling was even faster and easier if horses were harnessed to a carriage or wagon, and within a short period of time all sorts of horse-drawn vehicles were developed, ranging from heavy carts to lightweight war chariots. As with all developments, people in different regions progressed according to their specific needs and environment, although it is likely that many discoveries and inventions took place in different areas simultaneously.

As travel between countries became more common, so horses began to be imported from their native regions. It became apparent that different types were suitable for different tasks, and the types began to be crossed to produce new and different animals. The heavier European breeds formed the basis for the Medieval warhorses, while lighter animals were found more suitable for riding, pack, and carriage work. Eventually, over the centuries, breeds were produced for single, specific tasks, and refining and improvement has been carried out to such an extent that it is almost impossible to recognize the original ancient types in the modern and sophisticated horse breeds of today.

Horse Types

Every modern breed owes its existence to one or more of the three recognized ancient horse types. The distinct identity of each type may have been blurred as cross-breeding has fused different characteristics within different breeds, but these three types form the basis of every horse breed known today. Of the three, two still exist in some form, while the third is now extinct.

The Asiatic Wild Horse (Equus caballus Przewalski) is also known today as Przewalski's Horse, after the 19th century Polish explorer who discovered a herd

HORSES GRAZING AT MOUNT TAIHENG, CHINA

of wild horses in Mongolia in 1879. The Asiatic Wild Horse roamed the plains and steppes of Asia and still exists in the wild in certain, controlled areas to this day, although it is most usually found in zoos. This horse is relatively small and solid, standing just over four feet tall (13 hands), and is dun-colored with darker mane, tail, and legs.

The Tarpan (Equus caballus gmelini) originated across eastern Europe and parts of the former Soviet Union. Its name, Tarpan, although often used as a breed name today, is really a name given to horses exhibiting a certain set of characteristics, typical of wild horses from this region. The original Tarpan horses are believed to have become extinct. Those that exist today are thanks to intensive research and a cross-breeding process involving local mares and Przewalski stallions. The Tarpan is similar in size to the Asiatic Wild Horse, but not quite as stocky. Their coloring is coarse gray, often with darker heads.

The Diluvial Horse (Equus caballus sylvaticus) is now extinct. The larger, heavier Diluvial, or Forest Horse as it is also called, originated in northern Europe. It is widely accepted as being the forerunner for the heavy horse breeds found today.

However, it also accepted that there was a further division among horse types that occurred shortly before horses were domesticated for the first time. This division split the three ancient horse types into four, forming two pony types (1 and 2), and two horse types (3 and 4).

Pony Type 1
A small pony type, around four feet tall (12 hands), similar in appearance and characteristics to the Exmoor Pony. This type is thought to have evolved from the Tarpan, and developed in the northwest of Europe. It was a hardy type, capable of enduring extreme cold and damp conditions.

Pony Type 2
Taller than Pony Type 1, at around four feet, four inches (14 hands), Pony Type 2 was also stockier and heavier. It was found in far northern Europe and parts of Asia. This type probably originated from the Asiatic Wild Horse, and would have been similar to today's Norwegian Fjord.

Horse Type 3
Taller and of lighter build than the two Pony Types, Horse Type 3 stood between four feet eight inches and five feet (14.2 and 15 hands) tall. It developed in Central Asia, from the Tarpan, and its hardiness helped it survive in extreme dry and arid conditions. Its closest equivalent today is the Akhal-Teke.

Horse Type 4
This was the lightest and finest built Horse Type. Smaller than Type 3, but once again probably developed from the Tarpan, it originated in western Asia, and is

AKHAL TEKE IN RUSSIA

widely regarded as being the forebear of today's Arab horse, which itself is believed to have influenced more modern breeds than any other horse. However, it would most closely have resembled today's Caspian Horse.

The Development of Modern Horse Breeds

The breeds that have developed in different parts of the world have largely inherited the characteristics of one or more Horse or Pony Type, depending on where they originated. Certain breeds today have been heavily influenced by Oriental horses for example, while others owe more to European-based types.

Although cross-breeding between types has blurred the distinctions in many respects, horses can still be generally classified by type today. Three main types exist. These are Light Horses, commonly known as Warmbloods, Heavy Horses, known as Coldbloods, and Ponies. Ponies are generally defined as being less than 15 hands tall, with stockier proportions than the Horse. However, disagreements as to whether a particular breed constitutes a Horse or Pony do sometimes occur.

Horse breeding has been carried out for centuries, and would originally have been done in order to maintain herd numbers. Horses that breed in the wild are more at risk from illness, accident, or predators, so man would have taken care to protect their newly domesticated herds. Breeding in this way would have continued for centuries, with breed purity largely being maintained, except where natural cross-breeding, between wild and domesticated horses, occurred.

WESTFALIAN WARMBLOOD

However, as travel between countries became more common, and people were introduced to breeds from different regions, the desire to duplicate these new breeds arose, followed inevitably by the desire to improve on existing breeds. Characteristics of the different types were gradually mixed and refined through cross and inter-breeding over the centuries. Horses have been, and continue to be, bred for specific purposes, and new and changing requirements call for a specific set of characteristics. Careful selection is carried out, so that a horse that exhibits certain of the required traits can be mated with one that has the remaining traits. Or horses of similar traits are mated to strengthen those characteristics in the resulting progeny. The result should be a breed that possesses all the desirable characteristics. Finally, cross-breeding is also done to refine or improve existing breeds. To lighten a heavy horse, for example, blood will be introduced from a lighter breed.

There are dangers inherent in breeding programs however. Some breeds do not mix well, while others possess traits which, when mixed, can produce congenital defects, or weaknesses. As with excessive dog breeding, there is the risk that too much breeding can produce an animal that is almost a freak, poor in health and suitable for no purpose other than decoration or novelty. Several such examples unfortunately exist in the dog world, although things are not so bad at present with horse breeding. The closest example must be the Miniature Horse, which has been successively bred down to such a tiny size that it is like a toy breed. Fortunately most types of miniatures are reasonably healthy animals, although several do exhibit physical weaknesses.

Today, most horses are domesticated breeds. Herds of wild horses can still be found, mainly in remote areas, such as Przewalski's Horse, but it is widely accepted that many of the breeds that we refer to as "wild" today are not truly so. Rather, they are the progeny of domesticated breeds that have returned to the wild, having escaped or been abandoned by their owners. Often horses from different breeds will herd together, and cross-breed, forming a sort of "mongrel" breed. Over the years these feral horses have also adapted to survive in their new environment, becoming coarser and hardier, and less like their domesticated forebears. A typical example of such a feral horse is the Mustang, found throughout North America. Various types of Mustang can be found in different parts of the continent. Some of these are actually classified as separate, more purebred breeds, but, in general, the common Mustang is an amalgam of many horse breeds.

Breed Conformation

To classify and register as belonging to a particular breed, a horse must display the conformation laid down as standard for that breed. Conformation can basically be defined as the structure of the horse: its physique, characteristics, and attributes. As a breed is officially recognized, its conformation is registered, and only horses conforming to these standards will be accepted by the registry organizations. As breeds develop, entry requirements often become increasingly stringent, with even the most minor variation causing a horse to be disallowed.

MUSTANG

USA SHOWHORSE

The conformation of each breed depends primarily on its intended purpose. A horse intended for draft work for example, must conform to certain standards relating to musculature, power, and bulk. The requirements for a racehorse, on the other hand, will be completely different, with lightness and speed being prime objectives. However, balance is considered the most important factor in the conformation of all horse breeds.

It is the physical proportions of the horse that determine most of its characteristics. A well-proportioned horse, whether of a light or heavy build, will naturally be healthier and more able to work well than a horse of ungainly proportions. The proportions of certain parts of the body are also important. Where speed is considered essential, in a racehorse for example, a long neck and relatively short back are necessary. However, for a draft horse, which is of much heavier build, a long neck would be a liability. A broad, short, well-muscled neck is needed to keep the animal in proportion.

In essence then, good conformation requires a well-proportioned body, head, and limbs. This in turn gives the horse a good, balanced stance.

Breed Characteristics

The physical structure, or conformation of the horse, is not the only criterion which determines whether a horse will be allowed to register as a particular breed. Coat coloration is also important, with certain breeds allowing a restricted range of colors, while others allow almost any color. Patterns or markings can also be a deciding factor. Some breeds allow no markings, while others depend on it. The color of the mane and tail is also often a criterion. In fact, some breeds are known as "color" breeds. That is, the physical conformation of the horse is of minor importance (although good proportions will always play a part). It is the coat color and markings that allow or disallow registration within the breed. A famous example of such a breed is the Pinto. Horses of various pedigrees are classified as Pintos, as long as their patterns conform to breed standards.

Height can also be a primary breed criterion. The best-known example of a "height" breed is the American Miniature. Again, pedigree is relatively unimportant, and horses from all bloodlines are accepted, as long as they meet the strict maximum height restriction.

Certain breeds also require something more from their horses. These are the "gaited" breeds, where the horse must exhibit one or more rhythmic paces, or gaits, in order to qualify. Such breeds include the Puerto Rican Paso Fino and the Peruvian Paso.

In general, however, breed characteristics are determined by the particular task the horse is intended to perform. Show horses and sports horses, for example, have strict criteria regarding the level of attractiveness of qualifying horses both in terms of general appearance and color. Heavy work horses, on the other hand, are primarily judged on their build and strength.

Temperament and intelligence are also important to varying degrees within breeds. A show horse, which must regularly perform a series of agile movements, and which must react quickly to commands from its owner, must, by necessity, be quick-witted and high-spirited. A horse intended for farm work will in the same way, be most useful if it is docile and somewhat dull; able to carry out slow and steady work with little change or variation.

SOVIET HEAVY DRAFT HORESE

Stamina and hardiness are also major criteria for different breeds. Horses that will be used for long distance riding over harsh terrains will need to be extremely hardy, as conditions dictate that they must be able to fend for themselves if necessary. This is in contrast to racehorses for example, which although needing to exhibit speed and agility, do not need to be hardy, as they are cared for in the lap of luxury.

It is clear to see therefore, that breed regulations have developed according to the purpose of the particular breeds, and each set of criteria is tailored according to the requirements of each breed.

Tracing Today's Breeds

The three main, ancient horse types developed in different parts of the world, each evolving particular characteristics, depending on their local environment. As these types evolved, a certain number of distinctive breeds developed, and a small number of these became, in time, the forebears of today's breeds. Three of the earliest of these breeds have played a huge part in the development of almost every domesticated breed currently existing.

The first of these is the Arab, which originated from Far and Middle Eastern stock, and is widely regarded as having had the strongest influence on modern horse breeds. Some of the major modern breeds are Arab-based and today, traces of Arab blood can be found in horses on every continent. As well as playing such an important part in the development of other breeds, the Arab is still an important horse in its own right today.

GRONINGEN

The second important breed is the North African Barb. There are two schools of thought relating to the origins of the Barb. Some believe it is based on the Arab bloodline, and indeed the modern Barb will possess a degree of Arab blood. Another theory suggests that the Barb's origins lie with a group of horses that survived the Ice Age — a difficult theory to prove, but not an impossibility. Despite its great influence on many modern breeds, the Barb as a breed is much less well-known today.

The third most influential breed is the Andalusian, or Spanish Horse. The ancestry of this breed lies with the Barb. During the Moorish invasions of Iberia during the 8th to 15th centuries, Barb horses were imported into Spain and Portugal. Here they bred with the indigenous Iberian ponies to create the Andalusian breed. There is also a theory that the breed was, in fact, formed much earlier. This theory suggests that Barb horses may have traveled from North Africa to Spain across the land-link that was subsequently destroyed during the last great Ice Age. Once again this theory is impossible to prove, but it could well be that the Andalusian is a far more ancient breed than has been previously thought.

These, then, are the three early breeds that have undoubtably played the largest part in the development of modern horse breeds. However, in recent times a fourth breed, itself probably a mixture of all three principal breeds, although most likely predominantly Arab in origin, is making its mark. This is the English Thoroughbred, possibly the most influential breed in the world today. The Thoroughbred is used throughout the world to refine and improve almost every breed.

23

Although it becomes increasingly complicated when studying more recent breeds, which have considerably more mixed bloodlines, the path of development of many breeds is relatively easy to follow, and clear patterns can be seen to emerge in different parts of the world. Indeed it is possible to trace breed "maps" for many of the most important regional breeds, and these maps show how closely related many of today's breeds are.

The Americas

Although open to dispute, accepted thinking today maintains that horses became extinct in North America following the last Ice Age. It may well be that some managed to survive in the warmer climate of South America, and migrated northwards, but most probably the horse did not appear again in the Americas until being reintroduced by the Spanish who came to America in the 16th century. The first travelers who reached the shores of both South America and the southern parts of North America were the Conquistadores, an invading force who conquered and dominated the indigenous tribes. While the Conquistadores went on to fight for, and win, more lands, the next wave of Spanish visitors came to America. These were more peaceable in nature, being primarily settlers, carving a new home for themselves in the "New World."

The Spanish settlers brought with them their famed horses — the Andalusians. Over a period of time, a number of these horses escaped, or were abandoned, and these eventually formed huge herds that gradually traveled up

ANDALUSIAN

from South America and the southern states, into more northern regions of the North American continent. The principal descendent of these feral horses is the Mustang, varieties of which survive in the wild in America and Canada today, although in much reduced numbers. These Mustangs, with their Spanish ancestry, form the basis of many of today's American breeds.

As well as escaping into the wild, a number of Spanish horses were also captured by raiding parties of Native Americans. Many of these horses will have made their way into the ever-increasing herds of Mustang, but they also eventually formed the basis of some of America's other most famous breeds, including the Appaloosa and the Pinto (as well as the Paint Horse).

Spanish horses held sway in America for around a century, until new settlers, primarily from England, arrived in the 17th century. These settlers brought with them their own horses, the principal of these being the immediate forebear of the Thoroughbred, although the breed was not given this name until some time later. This Thoroughbred-type horse was descended almost solely from the Arab bloodline. Inevitably cross-breeding took place between the now native American-Spanish horses, and the Arab-based English breed. This cross eventually led to the breed we know as the Quarter Horse today.

The Quarter Horse, with its Arab and Spanish blood, in turn also formed the basis for the principal Canadian breed, the Canadian Cutting Horse.

The English Thoroughbred, and thus its Arab blood, also formed the basis of many of the other major American horse breeds, such as the Standardbred and the Morgan. The Arab influence is also responsible for the American Cream and White and the Saddlebred.

During the centuries that followed, new settlers arrived in North America, and these immigrants each brought with them their own horses. Over time, these

were also added to the breed mix, so some of today's breeds have a very color-ful heritage. However, it is plain to see that the most established breeds of American horses today owe their existence to two main bloodlines — the Spanish, or Andalusian, and the Arab. It is interesting to note that these types have developed separately, but almost simultaneously. The Spanish horse flourished mainly in the southern and western states of North America, forming generally stockier and hardier breeds of horse and pony, ideally suited for the warmer climate and dry plains and deserts of these regions. Having experienced the largest influx of Spanish settlers, it is little wonder that the predominant horse breed in South and Central America would be the Andalusian. Although crosses with other breeds have occurred in more recent times, the base bloodline of most of the main South American breeds remain Spanish.

The Arab influence began in the eastern states, forming more fine-boned and elegant breeds.

European Breeds

Northern European breeds can be loosely categorized into two types. The first is the heavier type of horse, descended from the ancient Diluvial type of northern Europe. One of the oldest of these types is the Belgian Brabant. Others include the English Shire, the French Percheron, and the Suffolk Punch. All these descen-dants of the ancient European horse, traditionally known as the Great Horse, in turn gave rise to more modern heavy draft breeds. These breeds were character-ized by their massive bulk, docility, and slowness. Additional infusions of blood from horses of Arab stock (the Thoroughbred was often used) produced a lighter horse, one which although capable of draft work, exhibited more speed and agility than its more stolid relations.

The second type of northern European horse is much lighter in build, and primarily used for riding or driving today. These horses, such as the Oldenburg and Trakehner (both from Germany) and the influential English Thoroughbred, all owe much to the Arab breed.

Horse breeds in the southern countries of Europe have generally developed from Spanish stock, which in turn means that their ancestry can be traced back to the Barb breed. Larger and heavier than the Arab, Barb-based breeds are still relatively light in comparison with the bulkier northern horses.

As with many breeds, however, crosses between horse types and breeds have produced various intermediate horse types. The German Wurttemburg, for example, was developed by crossing horses of Arab and Suffolk Punch lineage, which produced a powerful, but considerably less massive, horse. The Holstein (also from Germany) is an example where an originally heavy draft horse of "Great Horse" origin, was crossed with lighter breeds such as the Trakehner and Thoroughbred, to produce a completely different animal.

Many Eastern European and Russian breeds share a similar mixed ancestry, such as the Arab-based Caspian and Karabair and the heavier Russian and Vladimir Drafts.

SUFFOLKS

VLADIMIR HEAVY DRAFT HORSE

Oriental Breeds

Developing along different lines than the more famous Arab Horse, a distinct type of Oriental horse that exists today can trace its origins back to the Tarpan and Asiatic Wild Horse. These are the hardy mountain breeds of horse and pony that are mainly found in regions of China, Mongolia, and bordering countries of the former Soviet Union. Smaller and stockier in appearance than European breeds, these include the Bashkir, Zhemaichu, and Kazakh.

Australian Breeds

As with America, horse breeds in Australia are based on horses introduced into the country by settlers in the 18th century. Even the "wild" horse of Australia, the Brumby, is not an indigenous breed, but is actually descended from imported domesticated horses that escaped or were abandoned. Like the American

Mustang, Brumbies once roamed in great herds across Australia, although subsequent culling has reduced numbers drastically.

The Brumbies are descended from the forebears of Australia's main domesticated breed, the Australian Stock Horse, or Waler. The Waler is primarily Arab in origin, although there were later additions of European blood.

From this brief look at the origins of breeds, we can surmise how much of an influence the old breeds of Arab, Barb, and Spanish Horse have had in most parts of the world, and how most horses today can be traced back to the three original and ancient horse types.

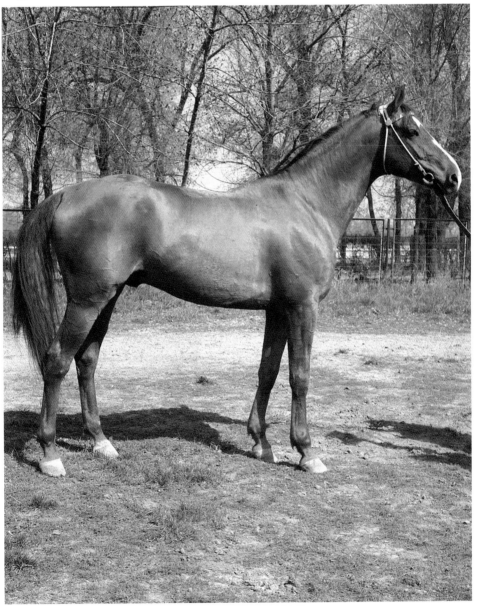

KUSTANAIR

The Horses by Country of Origin

SOVIET HEAVY DRAFT

Africa

ARAB

Origins: The Arab, together with the Mongolian horse, is a direct blood descendant of the horses of ancient times. The purity of the Arabian bloodline has influenced many of the other horse breeds worldwide — even Queen Victoria allowed her Arabian stallion to run wild for a period of time in the New Forest in the south of England in the hope that the local stock of ponies would be improved. Today, the Arab is considered the most important of the three early breeds that form the basis of most breeds today; the others being the Barb and the Andalusian.

Description: Horses that appear Arabian in type can be seen in illustrations that go back over 3,000 years. Arabians are known as hot-blooded horses, with eager and fiery natures, yet they are good-natured at the same time. Arab horses are widely regarded as being the most beautiful in the world. Their light frames and fine bones make them extremely graceful and elegant creatures. They are light-boned and quick, having beautiful concave or dished faces, with enormous eyes and wide foreheads. Although no bigger than 15 hands (5ft) and more often 14 hands (4ft 8in), the Arabian can carry large weights for long distances.

ARAB: USA

ARAB: MOROCCO

ARAB: UK

Argentina

CRIOLLO/CRIOULLO

Origins: The native horse of South America, the Criollo is related to the Spanish horses of the Conquistadores. Native Americans frequently raided the Spanish encampments, and many of these Spanish horses were stolen. Some were kept and bred, while others escaped and subsequently ran wild. Only the most adaptable horses were able to withstand the extremes of climate and the Criollo is outstanding, particularly in terms of toughness, a quality which made them favorites of the South American Gauchos. The Criollo also helped to found the Argentinean polo pony. Two famous Criollos were "Mancha" and "Gato," the horses that accompanied A. F. Tschiffely from Buenos Aires to New York — a journey of 13,350 miles — an expedition that was immortalized in the book *Tschiffely's Ride.*

Description: The Criollo has a long head and neck, with long and well-muscled legs. Its usual color is dun; height stands between 15 hands and 16 hands (5ft and 5 ft 4in).

CRIOLLO

FALABELLA

Origins: Despite its tiny size, the Falabella is a horse and not a pony, having clearly defined horse characteristics and proportions. Generally believed to be the smallest horse in the world, the breed was created near Buenos Aires by the Falabella family during the 19th century. Based on a cross between a Shetland Pony mare and a small Thoroughbred stallion, subsequent crossings with a careful selection of small horses, including further Thoroughbred as well as Arab blood, have resulted in the tiny horse we know today. The Falabella can be comparatively strong for its size, but due to substantial inbreeding, these horses are prone to congenital weaknesses, and are often quite delicate and weak. However, individual horses can be extremely long-lived and some have been recorded as living for over 40 years.

Description: The Falabella is a docile animal and takes all kinds of handling very well, making it ideally suited for one of its most popular uses, as a pet. Falabellas are also often bred as show animals. Due to possible inherited physical weaknesses, the Falabella requires a lot of care and attention to stay healthy. Horses of this breed have small heads, with a rather short, straight back and slim legs. Common colors are chestnut, bay, and black, and Appaloosa patterns and markings are not uncommon. The average height for a Falabella is around seven hands (28in).

Australia

AUSTRALIAN STOCK HORSE

Origins: Also known as the Waler. A crossbreed, the Waler is a mixture of the breeds that existed in colonial Australia. The name is derived from New South Waler; a horse bred in New South Wales, Australia's first colony. The foundation stock was based on animals from the Cape of Good Hope and, later, English horses such as Thoroughbreds, Clydesdales, and Timor ponies (interestingly, some of latter, the last in existence, are said to live in the Kimberley area).

The Waler was used as a remount for the British army in India. Rajahs also bought them for military uses and as polo ponies. Their endurance as remounts for the Australian army became legendary during the Boer War and during World War I. From this base stock, more outcrosses were made during the later 20th century and the Australian Stock Horse Society includes Appaloosas, Thoroughbreds, and Arabians in their stud book to produce the horse now known as the Australian Stock Horse.

Description: This horse looks very different from the original Waler. Used on farms and sheep stations, it also makes a good eventer and polo pony. The Australian Stock Horse has a long neck and body, a deep chest, and a well-muscled frame. Legs are long and slim, but also well-muscled. Height varies between 14 hands and 16 hands (4ft 8in and 5ft 4in). All colors are allowed.

BRUMBY

Origins: The Brumby is the wild horse of Australia. Usually of mixed blood, its origins can be traced back to the mid-19th century, during the time of the Australian gold rush. At this time many horses were abandoned, or escaped, eventually forming herds. They adapted to their surroundings, and can now be found in two distinct environments. Toughest of the lot is the desert type, found in outback Australia. There they have to contend with drought, flood, and extremes of temperature. The mountain Brumby, however, has access to plenty of water and grasslands.

Description: Reversion to the wild has meant that only the toughest horses could survive, and those that have thrived in the feral herds have changed in order to adapt to their environment, becoming stockier and coarser than their domesticated forebears. Brumbies have sturdy bodies, somewhat heavy heads, and strong feet. Coat coloration can include any solid color and height stands at around 15 hands (5 ft).

AUSTRALIAN STOCK HORSE

Austria

LIPIZZANER

Origins: The name Lipizzaner immediately brings to mind images of the elegant Spanish Riding School of Vienna, so called because the founding stallions were from Spain. The Spanish were acknowledged as fine breeders of horses and during the 16th and 17th centuries it became fashionable for royal courts to import them. The Lipizzaner breed was founded in 1580 by the Archduke Charles II, son of Ferdinand I, who chose Lipizza or Lipica as the base for the new stud farm. Nine stallions and 24 mares were imported from Spain and bred with selected local horses. The stud flourished and more imports were made from Italy, Denmark, and Germany. After the end of the Austro-Hungarian Empire, the Austrian school stud was moved to Piber in southern Austria. Lipizza came back into its own again when it became part of Yugoslavia at the end of World War II. Piber itself had been taken over by Germany and the Lipizzaner mares were sent to Bohemia from where they were rescued by the US Army and returned at the end of the war.

To this day Lipizzaner stallions are named for six sires of the late 18th century: "Pluto," "Conversano," "Neopolitano," "Favory," "Maestoso," and "Siglavy." The Austrian Lipizzaners go through a three-year training period leading up to the exercises known as the "schools on the ground" and the "schools above the ground;" the movements of *Haute Ecole*. Hungarian and Yugoslavian Lipizzaners are also trained as dressage and harness horses.

Description: Lipizzaners have longer than average heads and a distinctive arched neck. The back is long and often slightly hollow, and the legs are sturdy and well-formed. The Lipizzaner is intelligent, usually gray in color, and has a reputation for longevity; their height is between 15 hands and 16 hands (5ft and 5ft 4in).

NORIKER

NORIKER

Origins: The name Noriker is a corruption of Noricum, what the Romans called the region of today's Austria. It became the best known of the Alpine workhorses, evolving into a general purpose workhorse (it is still used as an army horse and as a light draft horse). In the 16th century, the breed was refined using infusions of Italian and Spanish blood — Andalusian in particular. Further cross-breeding took place in the 19th century, with additions of Holstein, Cleveland, and Oldenburg blood, among others.

Description: One of the requirements of the Noriker stud book, registered in 1903, is that the girth should be not less than 60 percent of the height at the withers; this makes for an exceptionally deep body. Today's Noriker is a strong and calm animal, with a heavy head, distinctive long mane, and a wide chest. Its legs are somewhat short, but very well muscled. The usual colors are chestnut, brown, or black. Another version — the Pinzgauer-Noriker — is distinct in that it is a spotted horse. Average height stands at around 15.2 to 16.2 hands (5 ft 1in to 5 ft 5in).

Belgium

ARDENNAIS

ARDENNAIS

Origins: An ancient breed that was used by the Romans for prized warhorses, the Ardennes comes from France and Belgium. An infusion of Arab blood during the 18th century gave the Ardennes a more refined appearance. These horses possess great stamina and endurance, traits that brought the breed to the attention of Napoleon, who frequently utilized them in military campaigns. Later they were used as cavalry horses and as artillery wheelers during World War I.

Description: The breed has seen several changes in its history, including attempts to make it larger by crossing it with the Brabant. The Ardennes is noted for its hardiness and for being economical to feed. It has a small, straight, but rather heavy head and a short, stocky body, short legs, and broad feet. It is popular in other countries than Belgium, especially Sweden, where a smaller version exists. Roan is

the usual color. Height stands at 15 hands to 16 hands (5ft to 5ft 4in).

BELGIAN HALF-BLOOD

Origins: Also known as the Belgian Warmblood. Development of the Half-blood began shortly after World War II, and it was intended for use in competition work as an alternative to Belgian heavy breeds. To achieve this, the lightest of the heavy breeds was crossed with imported stock from France — the Selle Français, Arab, and Thoroughbred proved most influential. Belgian Half-bloods of recent years have performed well in events such as show jumping. Their fame has spread over recent years and they are so widely regarded as excellent competition horses that they are a popular Belgian export.

Description: The head is alert and refined, with a long neck and sloping shoulders. Much emphasis is placed on the straightness of limbs and

41

soundness of feet. The breed is noted for having a willing temperament. Coat coloration includes all solid colors and average height is around 15.2 to 16.2 hands (5ft 1in to 5ft 5ins).

BRABANT

Origins: Also known as Belgian Draft Horse. The Brabant is believed to be able to trace its ancestry back to the prehistoric horses that once roamed this region. This is a breed that, since the beginning of the 20th century, has hardly ever been influenced by outside bloodlines. Many examples have been exported worldwide, particularly to the United States. There are three versions of the breed: Big Horse of the Dendre, Gray Horse of Nivelles, and Colossal Horse of Mehaique.

Description: The breed survives in large numbers today and is noted for the strength of its massive shoulders and quarters, making it well-suited for all kinds of heavy draft and farm work. It has a very calm, almost passive, temperament, and works slowly but willingly. Its usual coloring is chestnut or roan. Height is 16 hands to 17 hands (5ft 4in to 5ft 8in).

BRABANT

Brazil

CAMPOLINA

Origins: The Campolina, breed was founded in 1870 by Cassiano Campolina on his farm in Brazil. His crossing of a black mare of Barb blood, with a pure Andalusian stallion produced "Monarca," a dark gray colt who can be said to be the father of the Campolina breed. The breed has been improved and adapted over the years by the infusion of blood from other breeds, including the Clydesdale, Holsteiner, and most notably the Mangalarga Marchador. However, in 1834, the breed standard was set, and no further crossing was accepted.

Description: Today the Campolina is used as a light draft horse. Heavy and stockier than its Mangalarga relatives, like the latter, the Campolina has a long head, long legs, and a short back.

It is quite a hardy animal and is often used for long-distance riding. It has an even temperament and trains well. Campolina height stands at an average of 15 hands (5ft), and coat coloration can vary from gray to bay or sorrel.

MANGALARGA

Origins: Developed in the 19th century, the Mangalarga is based on the crossing of an imported Portuguese stallion with native Brazilian mares of Spanish extraction. Almost from the beginning, purity of the breed was considered important, and over the years very little cross-breeding has taken place. The breed is also known by the extended name of Mangalarga Marchador. This name comes from the breed's distinctive gait, known as the marcha. This is a smooth, fast, rhythmic step, and the Mangalarga can maintain the marcha for long distances. As well as the convenience of covering plenty of ground in a short time, the marcha also offers considerable comfort to the rider.

Description: The Mangalarga is a hardy and versatile breed, capable of adapting to all kinds of climates and environments, and quick to learn new skills. It is a docile and intelligent animal, with an even temperament which makes it extremely easy to train. The Mangalarga build is relatively light, but very strong. It is primarily used as a ranching or riding horse, but is also used for light farm work. The Mangalarga has long legs, tough feet, and powerful muscles. Coat color is solid and generally bay, chestnut, gray, and roan. Average height stands at around 15 hands (5ft).

MANGALARGA

Canada

CANADIAN CUTTING HORSE

Origins: It is believed that the Canadian Cutting Horse can trace its ancestry back to the horses sent from France by Louis XIV in the 16th century. This primarily Arab and Andalusian blood was mixed over the centuries by cross-breeding, principally with the Quarter Horse, which the Canadian horse strongly resembles.

Description: Somewhat larger than the Quarter Horse, the Canadian Cutting Horse retains many of its characteristics, such as strength, agility, and speed. Its intelligence, hardiness, and its easy adaptability to training makes this horse the perfect ranching mount — hence its name. These characteristics also make the Canadian Cutting Horse an excellent competitor in rodeos and shows. The Canadian Cutting Horse is good-natured and energetic, not prone to nervousness. It has a broad chest, wide shoulders, and well-muscled legs that are often a little short and stocky in appearance. Generally black, dark brown, bay, or chestnut, Canadian Cutting Horses can stand between 14 to 16.1 hands (4ft 8ins to 5ft 4ins).

Czech Republic

KLADRUBER

Origins: Also known as Kladruby. Developed at the Kladrub stud in the former Bohemia during the 16th century, the Kladruber is based on Italian and Spanish horses imported into Bohemia by Emperor Maximilian II. The original cross involved Barbs and Turks with Alpine horses, with later infusions of Andalusian and Lipizzaner blood. The Kladruber breeding program was extremely selective, with horses specifically intended for show as carriage or parade horses. Two colors of

Kladruber were originally bred; gray and black. The black type came under serious threat in 1930 when many were sent to be slaughtered for meat. Fortunately some black mares survived, and today both colors are thriving once more. The Kladruber can still be found in parades and shows the world over, and they also make excellent sport driving horses.

Description: Kladrubers are strong and energetic animals, with a docile and friendly temperament. The Kladruber has a long head with a broad forehead. Its neck is long and generally arched, and it has long, well-proportioned legs. Average height stands at around 16.2 to 17 hands (5ft 5ins to 5ft 8ins).

Chile

CHILEAN CORRALERO

Origins: As with many horse breeds of Central and South America, the Chilean Corralero's ancestry can be traced to the Spanish horses brought to the country by the Conquistadores during the 16th century. Chilean breeds began with the arrival of the new governor, Mendoza, who arrived in Chile in 1557 and brought with him 42 prime horses. By the beginning of the 19th century, a pure Chilean breed had already developed, and the Corralero made its first appearance at the end of the same century.

Chilean horses have been, first and foremost, work horses. Used as warhorses since the time of the Spanish Conquistadores, they have also been indispensable for farming, cattle herding, and as means of transport. Today, the Chilean Corralero also often features in rodeos, giving this versatile, agile, and intelligent horse a perfect opportunity to shine.

Description: The characteristics of the Chilean Corralero are a proportional flat head with small and separated ears. Eyes and nasal apertures must go behind the facial profile and the horse must possess a fine, small muzzle and an abundant mane. It has a broad and deep chest, a voluminous center, arched ribs, full and short flanks, rounded hindquarters, a hard musculature, and short extremities. The Chilean Corralero is generally very well-proportioned and well-muscled. Graceful but sturdy it stands at around 14 hands (4ft 8ins).

China

HEQU

Origins: Also known as Nanfan. A native of the Chinese Qinghai Province, the Hequ was also known as the Nanfan until the middle of this century. However, this caused confusion as Nanfan is also another name given to the Tibetan pony, a completely different animal. The origins of the Hequ stretch back to the period between the 7th and 10th centuries known as the T'ang dynasty. The emperor of the time wished to produce a breed suitable to be used as a cavalry horse. He instituted a major breeding program, importing horses from across Asia to cross with Tibetan stock. Infusions of Mongolian blood came about during Mongolian invasions several centuries later.

Description: The Hequ is, by necessity, a hardy animal, as its home is high in the mountains where temperatures are often low and terrain is rough. It is a strong and sturdy animal, and is therefore ideally suited for its main uses as a riding and pack horse. There are three main types of Hequ horse, found in different areas of the Province. The Jiaode is generally coarser in appearance and build, and its not as powerful as its relatives. The Suoke has a larger head than the other types, while the Kesheng breeds closely with Mongolian horses, so is not as pure-bred. Hequ horses are usually brown, black, or gray, and height can reach 13.3 hands (4ft 5ins).

SANHE

Origins: For many centuries, the grassland in the region of China known as the Inner Mongolia Autonomous Region was renowned for the superior horses bred by the native nomadic tribes. Many of these horses were considered so fine that they were prized by emperors and used as cavalry horses in the royal armies. During the early 18th century, a particularly fine breed was developed, known as the Soulun. Elegant and attractive in appearance, and with excellent handling, they were ideal cavalry mounts. The Soulun formed the basis for the later breed known as the Sanhe. At the beginning of the 20th century, settlers began to arrive in the area from Russia, and they brought with them their own horse breeds, including the Orlov. Later, during World War II, the occupying Japanese developed a stud in the region, including Arab, Thoroughbred, and American Trotter horses. These influxes of different breeds inevitably resulted in a degree of cross-breeding, and official studies carried out about ten years after the end of the war led to the formation of two new studs specifically to develop the subsequent Sanhe breed. Today the Sanhe is generally used for riding, both for pleasure and sport, and for light harness work.

Description: The Sanhe is widely believed to be the most well-developed of Chinese horse breeds and although stocky and well-muscled, it has an attractive appearance. The Sanhe coat is usually bay or chestnut.

WILD HORSES IN NATURE RESERVE, XINJIANG

Denmark

DANISH WARMBLOOD

Origins: The Danish Warmblood is one of the most recent of the world's horse breeds, as its stud book was only officially opened in the 1960s. Ironically, it was developed from one of Denmark's most ancient breeds, the Frederiksborg. Horse breeding is very much an ancient Danish tradition but, in spite of this, the Danes found themselves relying on imported riding horses for a considerable period after World War II. Subsequently, using the Frederiksborg as foundation stock, a careful breeding program was started. The first crosses were with Thoroughbreds, then Trakehners and Anglo-Normans. The result is an enviable competition horse, an example of which won the silver medal for dressage in the 1984 Olympic Games.

Description: The Danish Warmblood is similar in looks to the Thoroughbred. In conformation, everything looks near perfect: the head is intelligent while the body has great strength with excellent limbs. The Danish Warmblood is bred by private breeders, who have between them produced horses capable of winning many of the major dressage and three-day events. Many are now also exported abroad. The Danish Warmblood is an intelligent horse with a kindly nature. All solid colors are permissible, but bay is common. Height stands between 15.3 hands and 17 hands (5ft 1in and 5ft 8in).

FREDERIKSBORG

Origins: King Frederik of Denmark was an enthusiastic horse breeder and in 1562 he founded the stud farm that was to bear his name. Andalusian horses were one of the first of the foundation breeds. At that time every European royal court had its own equine high school that could perform dressage and exhibit skill at arms before guests. The Frederiksborg excelled at such events and was also unbeatable as a saddle, harness, and cavalry horse. A Frederiksborg stallion was even used to improve the most famous of the high school breeds, the Lipizzaner.

Later, during the 19th century, Frederiksborgs were crossed with Eastern and British half-bred stallions, further improving these excellent horses. Indeed, the quality and popularity of the Frederiksborg was so great that it very nearly brought about the extinction of the breed. Many of the finest horses were exported and breeding stocks were heavily depleted resulting in much poorer examples (although this could also be blamed on an attempt to breed lighter animals more like the Thoroughbred in looks). The royal stud was forced to close after 300 years of successful work and it was left to private breeders to carry on. Danish breeders are now trying very hard to preserve the original Frederiksborg.

Description: The head of the Frederiksborg could hardly be called handsome: it is large with big ears, but it does have an intelligent look. The body is long with powerful shoulders that aid the horse's high action. Chestnut is the most usual color and height stands at 15.3 hands to 16 hands (5ft 1in to 5ft 4in).

JUTLAND

Origins: Denmark's breed of heavy horse is named after its home region of Jutland where it has been bred for centuries. From Jutland it traveled to the other Danish islands and found great favor as a warhorse in medieval times. The modern Jutland began to emerge during the 19th century when it was crossed with British breeds such as the Cleveland Bay and Suffolk Punch. The best stallion lines are related to "Aldup Munkedal," "Fjandbo," and "Lune Dux."

Description: The Suffolk Punch influence can be seen in the shape of the Jutland. It also has marked similarities to the Schleswig Heavy Draft horse, as

they have ancestry in common — both breeds having been influenced by the Suffolk Punch stallion, "Oppenheim LXII." The Jutland has a massive build, with a short neck, short thick legs, and wide heavy feet. The usual color is chestnut, but roan is also seen. Height stands between 15 hands and 16 hands (5ft and 5ft 4in).

KNABSTRUP

Origins: The Knabstrup is bred specifically for its unusual spotted coat. History tells us that the breed developed from one mare, called "Flaebehoppen," left in Denmark by a Spanish officer during the Napoleonic Wars. Used by a butcher named Flaebe on his delivery round, the mare was noticed by Major Villars Lunn, owner of the Knabstrup estate and a keen riding horse breeder whose stock was based on the Frederiksborg. Lunn admired the mare's chestnut coat which had "blanket" markings and a white mane and tail. He bought her

and began a breeding program for a line of spotted horses. In 1812, she was mated with a Palomino Frederiksborg stallion, and produced a colt named "Flaebehingsten." It was rumored that the colt's coat had "more than 20 colors."

Description: Much cross-breeding has taken place since then to produce different color patterns. This caused the breed's conformation to suffer at one time, but the modern Knabstrup is an animal of great quality, similar to the Appaloosa. Due to the large amount of cross-breeding that has always occurred to improve pattern, there is little physically that defines the Knabstrup — it is almost entirely a color breed. However, in general the Knabstrup is a well-proportioned horse, although somewhat stocky in build. Kind and gentle, very strong, and a good riding horse, the breed is very popular in the circus. Height stands at 15.2 hands to 16 hands (5ft 1in to 5ft 4in).

KNABSTRUP

Europe

PRZEWALSKI

Origins: Also known as the Mongolian or Asian Wild Horse. Discovered by Russian explorer Colonel N. M. Przewalski in 1881, it is unlikely that many of these ancient ponies survive in the wild today. However, numbers of them were once found in the Tachin Schara Nuru Mountains at the edge of the Gobi Desert. It was thought that this breed was the common stock from which all horses were descended. We now know this is not the case; that honor must go to the sole surviving breed of a type of horse known as the Plateau Horse, which was one of four ancient ranges of horse to survive the

Ice Age. Early cave paintings, however, do show men hunting creatures very similar to the Przewalski.

Description: Przewalski horses are strongly built and thickset with a heavy head on a short neck. A hardy and enduring animal, groups survived for many years in Mongolia. The Przewalski has no forelock and a short almost hogged mane. Sandy, black, or dun are the usual colors, often with a black stripe down the center of the back. The Mongolian and Chinese type of ponies are direct descendants of the Przewalski. A small horse breed, the Przewalski stands between 12.2 and 14.2 hands (4ft 1in and 4ft 9in).

Finland

FINNISH

Origins: Often known as the Universal due to its adaptability for many kinds of work, the Finnish horse is based on crosses between native ponies and a variety of other horse breeds. The Finnish horse is a breed which splits into two distinctive types. Although small (height stands between 14.1 hands and 15.2 hands — 4ft 8in and 5ft 1in), one version is a powerful light draft horse, and the other, more lightly built animal, is used as a trotting or riding horse. Both are similar in conformation. Special breeding programs have been set up to refine the trotting horse for racing although the heavy horse is still the best way of hauling loads through the Finnish pine forests.

Description: A stud book was first opened for the Finnish horse in 1907; since then select breeding guidelines have been maintained. Although the head of the Finnish horse can be said to be plain, in appearance the breed is well proportioned and muscular, with a long mane and tail. It has a small, though heavy, head, sturdy legs, and a deep chest. The Finnish horse has a delightful temperament, steady and intelligent. They are a long-lived breed, well adapted to the extremes of the Scandinavian climate. Coat color is usually chestnut, gray, or bay.

FINNISH HORSE

France

BOULONNAIS

Origins: Originating in northwestern France, the Boulonnais breed was formed by the invading Romans during the 1st century AD. At that time they crossed the heavy French horses with their own horses; the more delicate Arabs. The result was a sturdy, compact, and almost elegant draft horse, which proved its worth as a warhorse for several centuries. Later cross-breeding also introduced Spanish, as well as more Arab blood. This has seen the development of the breed into the rather graceful heavy horse we know today. The breed name, Boulonnais, came into use during the 17th century. Extremely strong, this is a heavy draught horse, although nowadays it is primarily bred for meat.

Description: When crossed with other heavy horses, Boulonnais blood has been found to greatly improve the stock. Relatively energetic for a draft horse, the Boulonnais is quick to learn and possesses considerable stamina. It has a small head on a short neck, a wide chest, and short legs with particularly thickset thighs. It is well-proportioned and muscled. The coloration of the Boulonnais is generally grey, often dappled, although bay and chestnut can also be found. Height stands between 15.3 and 16.2 hands (5ft 1in and 5ft 5in).

BOULONNAIS

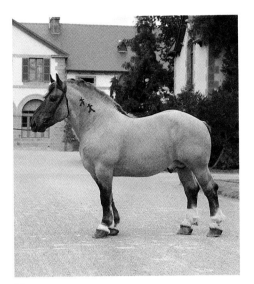

BRETON

Origins: There are several ideas relating to the original ancestry of the Breton. It has variously been described as descending from Asian breeds brought into Europe around 4,000 years ago, or from an indigenous small horse bred for centuries in Europe by the Celts. Whatever its lineage, ancestors of the Breton were almost certainly used as farming and warhorses during the Middle Ages. The modern Breton horse of northwest France was developed to meet a variety of demands, including farm work and transportation. At one time there were several types of Breton, used for heavy draft work, light draft work, and riding. The modern Breton breed is divided into a heavy draft type and a lighter type. The lighter of the two, the Postier Breton, is sometimes used as a coach horse. The heavier type was developed from crossbreeding with the Ardennes, Percheron, and Boulonnais and is still used as a workhorse.

Description: The head is square with a short thick neck. The body is short and strong with short limbs. The tail is usually docked. The usual colors are roan or chestnut. Height is 15 hands to 16 hands (5ft to 5ft 4in).

CAMARGUE

Origins: Ancestors of the Camargue are believed to date back to prehistoric times. Home for the Camargue horse is the swampy area between Aigues-Mortes and the Mediterranean. Known as the "White Horses of the Sea," the coat of the Camargue is always grey, although the foals are often born dark gray, brown, or even black. Since the 19th century, there has been considerable cross-breeding of the Camargue, with infusions of blood from the Arab, Barb, and English Thoroughbred. Care has been taken to foster and develop the breed in the latter part of the 20th century, as they had come dangerously close to extinction. The Camargue is necessarily hardy as most of its diet is of salty water and tough spiky grass. These horses are highly maneuverable at the gallop making them ideal for the job of working the famous Camargue black bulls in the bullring.

Description: The conformation of the Camargue is far from perfect as they tend to have an oversize head on a short neck. However, these horses have good bones and action as well as a short, strong back. Height stands at 13.2 to 14.2 hands (4ft 5in to 4ft 8in).

FRENCH TROTTER

Origins: Also known as the Norman Trotter. The development of this breed is linked to Harness racing, which gained popularity as a sport in France during the 19th century. In response to the demand for good trotting horses, breeders took Norman mares as their base stock and crossed them with suitable British breeds. Major influences were "Norfolk Phenomenon,"

an example of the forerunner of the Hackney, the now extinct Norfolk Trotter, and "Heir of Linne," a Thoroughbred. The resulting breeds were the Anglo-Norman and French Trotter; the latter being officially registered in 1922. American Trotter (Standardbred) blood was added later.

Description: The French Trotter is very strong, with more stamina than any other breed used purely for harness racing. The horse has powerful hindquarters with correspondingly hard and robust limbs. It has a graceful bearing with a fine head and neck. Its legs are slim but well-muscled and strong, and the feet can be quite soft. Coat coloration is most commonly chestnut, bay and black. The French Trotter can reach 16.1 hands (5ft 4ins).

NORMAN COB

Origins: The development of the Norman Cob began back in the 17th century, where it was produced to meet the requirement for a riding, light draft, and carriage horse. Largely bred at the studs of St Lì and Le Pin, both rightly famed for the wide variety of quality horses developed over several centuries, the Norman Cob today is somewhat heavier than its predecessors, but still largely used for farm work and transportation. It was given its name at the beginning of the 20th century due to its similarity in appearance to the English Cob.

Description: The distinctive appearance of the Norman Cob is mostly due to its docked tail. Today, although the practice is now illegal in England, Norman Cobs still have their tails

SELLE FRANÇAIS

docked. The Norman Cob is tough, very strong and active, and displays great stamina. It is also characterized by its stocky body, short back, and short, well-muscled legs. It is a friendly animal, very willing and hard-working. Coat coloration of the Norman Cob is usually bay or chestnut. Average height stands between 15.3 to 16.3 hands (5ft 1in to 5ft 6in).

PERCHERON

Origins: Based on the ancient indigenous breeds found in the Perche region of Normandy from which it takes its name, the Percheron has, over the centuries, received considerable infusions of Oriental and Spanish blood that can be clearly seen in its graceful bearing and fine features. This is one of the most popular of heavy horses, and can be found worldwide. There were originally two types, although today the lighter type is extremely rare. The breed was founded on the big Flemish horses and Arabians. In fact, the world's biggest horse was a Percheron, "Dr Le Gear," standing at 21 hands (7ft). Widely exported into Britain since World War I, the Percheron was once commonly used to pull the famous London omnibuses.

Description: For such a heavy horse the breed has a very free action. It is a strong breed, with great stamina and energy, as well as an even-temper. The head is intelligent and slightly Arabian-like; it is very deep chested with a compact body and the legs are short and well-muscled, with very little feathering. Usual colors are gray or black and height stands at 16 hands (5ft 4in) and upward.

SELLE FRANÇAIS

Origins: Descended from the ancient Norman breeds that had developed from the Arab horses imported into the country after the Crusades, and which are now sadly extinct, the modern-day Selle Français is one of the more recent of the French breeds. French breeders of the 18th and 19th centuries decided to refine the Norman horse with the introduction of Thoroughbred and Arabian blood. Its development was further improved during the period immediately after World War II and was influenced by the Norfolk Trotter. The Anglo-Norman was also a product of this selective breeding, as was the French Trotter. Bred in the area around Caen at Haras du Pin, the Anglo-Norman itself became a major influence on French regional breeds. As these breeds became more alike, it was decided to amalgamate them under one common name — Selle Français. The more heavyweight of them make good general riding horses. Others are used to great effect as competition horses and cross-country eventers.

Description: Standing at 16 hands (5ft 4in), the Selle Français is a strong, well-muscled horse, with powerful limbs and good bone. It is noted for having free and active paces. All solid colors are allowed, but chestnut is the most common.

Germany

BAVARIAN WARMBLOOD

Origins: Formerly known as the Rottaler, the Bavarian Warmblood was much in use as a warhorse, primarily during the Middle Ages. However, as with many of the older heavier breeds, a lighter blood was added during the 18th century. British horse breeds were a notable influence, the principal ones being the Thoroughbred and Cleveland Bay.

Description: The breed is now best known as a riding horse, but is also a successful competition horse, helped by considerable agility and calm temperament. Height stands at 16 hands (5ft 4in) and its usual color is chestnut.

EAST FRIESIAN

Origins: Before World War II, and the subsequent partition of Germany, the East Friesian had developed along such similar lines to the Oldenburg, that the two were considered almost the same breed. However, the political division of Germany also divided the two breeds, with the East Friesian being developed according to Eastern European breeding preferences. The East Friesian was refined using infusions of Arab blood, as well as incorporating crosses with stallions from the renowned Hungarian Balbolna stud. One of these stallions, Gazal, has played a significant part in the development of the breed.

EAST FRIESIAN

Today the East Friesian has been refined to such an extent that its origins are virtually unrecognizable. With the introduction of Hanoverian blood in more recent times, it is now a superior, light horse, used for both pleasure and competition riding, and occasionally for light draft work.

Description: The East Friesian is strong, good-natured and energetic, but requires care and maintenance to preserve its health. It is well-proportioned, with a long, often arched, neck, a deep chest, long back, and reasonably long legs which are well-muscled. Coat coloration includes most solid colors; generally brown, bay, chestnut, or black. Height stands at around 15.2 to 16.1 hands (5ft 5in).

HANOVERIAN

Origins: The most famous of the German breeds is the Hanoverian which has its origins in the German great horses of the Middle Ages. These heavyweight animals date from the pre-Christian era and can be traced back to a tribe called the Tencteri, who lived along the left bank of the Rhine. The Hanoverian continued as a warhorse until the use of armor died out. The breed was altered in 1735 when King George II of England founded the Celle stud. This was done to create a lighter farm and harness horse. Holstein stallions were crossed with the local mares, then English Thoroughbred blood was added. Subsequently, the "new" Hanoverian became popular as a coach horse. In 1867, Private breeders founded their own society with the intention of producing animals that could also be used as army horses. The requirements were changed again between the two world wars. At this time the emphasis was on an animal that could be used as a utility horse on the farm and as a

quality riding horse. The postwar years have seen the Hanoverian develop into an elegant competition horse.

Description: The Hanoverian is a strong and powerful horse with a showy action and a good temperament. Height stands between 16 hands and 17 hands (5ft 4in and 5ft 8in). All solid colors are accepted.

HOLSTEIN

Origins: The Holstein dates back to the 13th century when it was bred on good pasture ground along the banks of the Elbe River. It is believed to have Andalusian blood and some Oriental. During the 16th and 17th centuries, the breed became popular as a powerful riding and coach horse and many animals were exported abroad — particularly to France. The Holstein proved to be too heavy for military purposes and it was decided to refine the breed by the use of Thoroughbred blood, notably through the introduction of three Yorkshire Coach Horses in the 19th century. The resulting animal was one that was elegant enough for riding and driving, yet was strong enough for light farm work. A central stud, which stayed open until 1961, was formed in Traventhal and Holsteins were once again exported, many of them to South America. Numbers declined again after World War II as farms rapidly became mechanized and the Holstein was still considered too heavy as a competition animal. Again English Thoroughbreds were imported from Britain and consequently, the present day Holstein is a much lighter and elegant animal.

Description: The neck is long and arched with high withers and a strong back. Height stands at 16 hands to 17 hands (5ft 4in to 5ft 8in). All solid colors are permissible.

Mecklenburg

Origins: Similar in appearance to the larger Hanoverian, the Mecklenburg shares much of the same history. Its ancestors were much larger, heavier,

and very strong and were primarily used as warhorses. As warfare changed, and armor became outmoded, so the warhorse also underwent changes. Warmblood stock was introduced to create a lighter, superior horse, suitable for cavalry use. Its size and strength also made the Mecklenburg ideally suited as a light carriage horse. It retained this use up to World War II, although subsequent cross-breeding had produced a strong and agile riding horse, of medium build and considerable stamina. After World War II a breeding program was set up in East Germany which has produced the breed we know today. Some Anglo-Arab blood was introduced, and considerable crossing with Hanoverian stock took place. Used primarily as a riding and competition horse, the Mecklenburg also makes a suitable pleasure mount.

Description: A strong, yet docile breed, the Mecklenburg has a well-proportioned head on a long, strong

HOLSTEIN

neck. It has a long back, broad chest, strong, sturdy legs, and hard feet. Most solid colors occur, with brown, bay, or black being most common. Average height stands at 15.3 to 16 hands (5ft 1in to 5ft 4in).

OLDENBURG

Origins: Named for Count Anton von Oldenburg, this breed originated in northwest Germany. It used to be the heaviest of the German horses, related to the Friesian but, as with many other heavyweight breeds, much effort has been made to lighten it. Von Oldenburg was responsible for putting Spanish and Italian stock to the local mares in the 17th century. This result-ed in a powerful coach horse noted for maturing early. Later, in the 19th century, a breeders' society was estab-lished for the Oldenburg. At this time, a lighter horse was developed through the addition of Yorkshire Coach Horses, Thoroughbreds, Cleveland Bays, and Normans. These made superb coach horses that were also

capable of working as farm horses. Recent breeding programs using Thoroughbreds and Hanoverians have further refined the Oldenburg. At 16.2 hands to 17.2 hands (5ft 5in to 5ft 9in), the modern day Oldenburg is still Germany's tallest horse, and also one of the most powerful. Examples are now being used for competition work.

Description: Oldenburgs are known for having an even temperament with an elegant bearing. They have a well-proportioned head, strong neck and shoulders, and well-muscled legs. Limbs are short in relation to its deep and well-muscled body but with good bone. All solid colors are allowed.

RHINELAND HEAVY DRAFT

Origins: Also known as Rhenish-German. Based on the Ardennais and the Belgian Heavy Draft, the Rhineland Heavy Draft was developed in the middle of the 19th century and it was almost 100 years ago that the Rhenish stud book was founded. The best known sires were "Albion d'Hor," "Indien de Bievene," and "Lothar III." The breed quickly became a useful heavy draft horse, used by the farmers of Westphalia, Rhineland, and Saxony. Because of farm mechanization, there are very few examples of the Rhenish left today, and efforts are being made to produce a riding horse, the Rhinelander, using the heavy draft as foundation stock.

Description: The Rhenish is not unlike the Belgian Heavy Draught, with a plain head, short neck, short but well-muscled legs, and deep muscular body. It has a docile temperament and is hardy and hard-working. Height stands at 16 to 17 hands (5ft 4in to 5ft 8in) and the usual colors are chestnut and red roan.

SCHLESWIG HEAVY DRAFT

Origins: As with many European heavy draft horses, the powerful forebears of the Schleswig were used for centuries as warhorses for armored knights. The breed as we know it today was developed during the late 19th century to provide a heavy draft horse that could also be used by the military. Based on the Danish Jutland breed, it was strongly influenced by one stallion in particular, "Oppenheim LXII," a Suffolk Punch who also played a part in the development of the Jutland. As the beginning of the 20th century approached, Thoroughbred blood was introduced, to create a somewhat lighter draft horse. However, a variety of defects arose from this cross and later crosses with Breton and Boulonnais horses were intended to improve the breed once more. An amenable, strong, and reasonably fast horse, the Schleswig has been used primarily as a farm horse and for all kinds of transportation, including pulling heavy carriages.

Description: In appearance, the Schleswig somewhat resembles a cob, with a large head, short neck, and short, well-muscled legs. Coat color is generally a deep brown or chestnut, and height stands between 15.1 to 16.1 hands (5ft to 5ft 5in).

TRAKEHNER

Origins: The Trakehner has a fascinating history. Originally from East Prussia, the breed developed from the Schwieken, a tough little horse native to East Prussia. In 1732, Frederick William I of Prussia founded the Trakehnen Stud. He supplied an area of marshland in the northwestern area of East Prussia which was drained to become perfect pasture land. Frederick also donated horses from the royal studs and imported Arabians from Poland. Thoroughbred blood was added later, one of the most influential stallions being "Perfectionist," son of the famous race horse "Persimmon." Such careful breeding

RHINELAND HEAVY DRAFT

WESTFALIAN COLD BLOOD

produced an excellent riding horse, the pride of the German army. Only the best stallions were kept at the Trakehnen Stud and the three-year-olds were sent to the resident training stable and kept there for one year. As four-year-olds they underwent trials which included hunting with a pack of hounds and cross-country courses. Second best animals went to state stud farms, third class went to private breeders. The rest were used as remounts by the German army. This practice continued up to the end of World War I. In a drastic attempt to keep the best animals from the advancing Russian Army during this conflict a number were trekked across country to the west. The rest were left behind in what eventually became Poland, their famous stud destroyed.

Description: The Trakehner is good tempered with excellent conformation, very similar to the Thoroughbred. Height is 16 hands (5ft 4in), although taller examples are not uncommon. All solid colors are permissible.

WESTFALIAN

Origins: The modern Westfalian breed is based on a much older breed that dates back to the early 19th century and which was officially recognized in 1826. Over subsequent years, a selective breeding program took place for the purpose of refining the breed and in order to improve the horse's qualities as a riding and sports horse. This has involved infusions of English Thoroughbred, Arab, and Hanoverian blood. The combination of bloodlines eventually produced a fast, intelligent, powerful, and versatile horse, which has gone on to become a world-renowned competition breed. First reaching prominence as a high-class sports horse in the 1970s, Westfalians have won World Championships in 1978 and 1982, and have consistently performed to a high standard over the years. Westfalians are adaptable to several performance disciplines, including carriage driving and racing, although they principally excel at show jumping and dressage.

Description: Westfalians are high-spirited horses, although their even temperament makes them easy to train and they are very willing to learn. The main characteristics of the breed include a graceful bearing, lean lines, and a long back. Coat coloration can include any solid color and height stands between 15.2 to 16.2 hands (5ft 1in to 5ft 5in).

WÜRTTEMBURG

Origins: The Württemburg is bred at Germany's state-owned stud at Marbach, and can trace its ancestry back to the 16th century. This warmblood breed was founded when Arabian blood was mixed with German mares; later Anglo-Norman, Trakehner, and Suffolk Punch blood was added. The Anglo-Norman blood proved to be very important, and it is an Anglo-Norman that is credited with being the founder of the modern day Württemburg breed. However, the Trakehner has been an important influence in subsequent years, and this is the breed that is primarily used for refining the Württemburg today. The breed was originally intended as a light general purpose horse for farm and light draft work, but it is now extensively used extensively for competition work. It is also an excellent mount for both sport and pleasure riding.

Description: The Württemburg has good limbs, a long, straight back, and a sensible, intelligent head. It is an intelligent horse, quick to learn, and docile in temperament. It is a powerful horse, and possesses considerable stamina. The usual color is chestnut, but brown and bay are also common. Height stands at 16 hands (5ft 4in) and upward.

WÜRTTEMBURG

Great Britain

ANGLO-ARAB

Origins: The Anglo-Arab is a well-established breed based on the Arab and English Thoroughbred breeds. It originated in the UK although it is now particularly well known in France. Indeed, the French Anglo-Arab has been bred at stud farms for the last 150 years. The Anglo-Arab horse represents an amalgamation of the best qualities of both the Arabian and Thoroughbred breeds. It is more solid-looking than the Arabian, while being more Thoroughbred in appearance. Arabian blood has given more stamina and a spirited but kindly nature.

As the Anglo-Arab became a more popular riding horse in France, races especially for the breed were started. In later years, as the Anglo-Arab became more successful as a competition winner, a number were used to found the Selle Français. While not as fast as the Thoroughbred, the Anglo-Arab has excelled as a dressage, race, and competition horse.

Description: Today conformation of the Anglo-Arab is generally based on the French type, as these tend to be more consistent in appearance. The Anglo-Arab has a light frame, with a fine neck, and long back. Coat coloration can include most solid col-

ors, although brown tones are most common. Height standards have recently been changed from 15.3 hands (5ft 1in) to 16.1 hands (5ft 4in).

CLEVELAND BAY

Origins: The Cleveland Bay is the most ancient of the English horse breeds, originating in Yorkshire during the Middle Ages. Originally from Cleveland, the horse has been exported abroad in recent years to improve native stock and, at home, it is often used today as an ideal mating partner for the English Thoroughbred. For centuries the Clevelands have had two primary uses: as both agricultural workers and carriage horses, and it is still used for these purposes today. A Cleveland Bay/Thoroughbred cross also makes an ideal hunter. In England the Cleveland has often been used as a ceremonial carriage horse in displays and royal processions. As a farm horse, it has the advantage of being clean-legged (no feathering on the legs), unlike the larger heavy horses, and so works more quickly.

Description: Color should be bay or bay brown; the body wide with a deep girth and strong shoulders. The head should be large and convex in shape. The legs are comparatively short, although well-muscled and powerful, and the feet broad. Height is usually 16 hands to16.2 hands (5ft 4in to 5ft 5in). The Cleveland Bay is particularly noted for its stamina, presence, action, and intelligence. It has an even temperament and is an easy horse to train.

CLYDESDALE

Origins: One of Britain's heavy horses, the Clydesdale breed was founded in Lanarkshire. (Clydesdale is the old name for Lanarkshire.) Its foundation is believed to have been due to the

73

importation of a single Flemish stallion, although subsequent imports of both Flemish and Frisian stallions improved the breed and instilled it with more strength and bulk. Due to this, the 18th century saw considerable demand for use of the horse in the Scottish coalfields. The Clydesdale Horse Society was formed in 1877, and published its first stud book shortly afterwards. A popular horse, great numbers of Clydesdales have since been exported abroad.

Description: The usual colors are bay and brown, although black is also seen. White markings are allowed, and are most often seen on the legs and face. The most important aspects of the Clydesdale are its feet — which are broad — and limbs, which should be well-muscled. The Clydesdale has a long neck, often arched, deep chest, and well-built shoulders. The forehead is wide and open and the face flat. Clydesdales are very active movers for their size, and have a kind and gentle temperament. They are also very friendly horses, and have proved willing and quick learners. Heights range up to 16.2 hands (5ft 5in).

Cob

Origins: The Cob is a type rather than a breed of horse: a popular riding horse, well known for having a placid temperament and good manners. Although not particularly fast, it gives a comfortable, safe ride, and is a use-

CLYDESDALE

ful hunter, particularly for novice riders or the less mobile.

Description: The Cob is short-legged, with a deep body and small intelligent head on an arched neck. In the past it was fashionable to show the Cob with a hogged mane and docked tail. Tail docking is now illegal but many still prefer to show the horse with a hogged mane. Height should not exceed 15.2 hands (5ft 1in).

HACK

Origins: Not to be confused with the Hackney, the Hack, like the Cob, is a type, rather than a breed. A refined riding horse, many successful Hacks are Thoroughbreds so the conformation points of a good Thoroughbred also apply to the show Hack.

Description: The Hack must have perfect manners and stand absolutely still while the rider mounts and dismounts.

The breed society for the Hack is the British Show Hack and Cob Society. The height of these horses should be up to 15.3 hands (5ft 1in). Any color is allowed.

HACKNEY

Origins: With an ancestry that dates back to Danish horses first introduced to England during the 11th century, the Hackney is one of the oldest British breeds. Subsequently crossed with both native and Arab horses, these were the forebears of the Norfolk Trotter, from which today's Hackney is descended. The most famous of these old breeds was the Norfolk Roadster, an 18th century trotting horse, the most well-known example of which was the "Norfolk Cob," alleged to have done two miles in five minutes and four seconds.Hackneys have a mixture of Thoroughbred and Arabian blood.

Description: Hackneys are now mostly to be seen driving in the show ring. They have a long step, and a high-stepping trot, producing a pleasing gait that makes them ideal carriage horses. With this jaunty stride and high-set tail, the obvious impression of the Hackney is one of alertness. The perfect Hackney has a small head, long, arched neck, deep chest, and long, slim, and powerful legs. Usual colors are brown, chestnut, bay, and black.

HUNTER

Origins: The first hunting horses were required to carry people while they were hunting a number of different quarries. These days a Hunter is defined as a horse which is usually ridden with a pack of hounds, and over the years the best form of Hunter has evolved to suit this purpose. Notably, it has Thoroughbred blood, although horses as diverse as Shire Horses and ponies can also make good Hunters. The main criteria are a good conformation and action. The Hunter needs to be able to carry weight all day and over a variety of obstacles, if need be, during the season. So stamina and conformation are important. When being shown, Hunters are judged according to the weight that they will be asked to carry: lightweight, middleweight, and heavyweight. A separate category of Ladies' Hunters is also judged, and this type is ridden in the old-fashioned side-saddle manner. In the US, unlike Great Britain and Ireland, the horse will be asked to jump in the show ring, to prove its ability over fences.

HUNTER

Description: Although no breed defin-
ition exists, a Hunter should possess a
number of characteristics. These
include stamina, hardiness, and
power. A Hunter needs to be agile and
energetic, extremely obedient and
good-tempered, and should have an
even pace, whether at a walk, a trot,
or a gallop. Coat coloration can be
any solid color, and height can vary
according to primary breed type.

SHIRE

Origins: One of Great Britain's best
known and best loved heavy horses,
the Shire was originally bred in the
Huntingdon, Lincoln, and Cambridge
areas of England. It traces its beginnings to Elizabethan times and may
well be descended from an older
breed — the Great Horse of England
— as any horse in those times would
be required to carry a man in a suit of
armor, which could boost the weight
carried to about 450 pounds.
Although one of the slower breeds of
heavy horses (it can weigh around

2,000 pounds) the Shire can actually
pull loads of 10,000 pounds.
Fortunately, the breed avoided extinction despite the invention of the tractor
and it is still a popular sight at many
agricultural shows and plowing
matches with its harness decked out
with horse brasses and terrets.
Breweries still keep teams to haul their
drays for publicity purposes.

Description: The most common colors
are bay, brown, gray, or black.
Compared to the massive body size, a
Shire's head is rather small, while the
neck is long and arched. With long,
muscular and well-feathered legs,
height can be up to 18 hands (6ft). The
Shire has a gentle temperament.

SUFFOLK

Origins: Also commonly known as the
Suffolk Punch, the breed started in
Suffolk and is said to trace its roots
back to 1506. Modern examples can
all track their male bloodline back
directly to one horse, named "Blakes

Farmer," which was foaled in 1760. It is also one of the few breeds of heavy horse to have "clean" legs; that is to say, no feathering. This has the advantage of making the horse more active over heavy ground and making it easier to groom. The Suffolk is a handsome horse, does well on relatively poor feed and is long-lived: in working life they can live well over 20 years.

Description: A handsome animal, the Suffolk Punch is strong and compact in shape and has a small, elegant head. This conformation combined with short legs gives the horse a great deal of "pull." It is always chestnut in color, as are all the descendants of "Blakes Farmer," although there are obviously variations in the shade. In height the Suffolk stands at about 16 hands (5ft 4in) and it has a great width in front and in the quarters.

THOROUGHBRED

Origins: One of the best-known and most beautiful horses in the world. If anyone mentions the word racehorse, you will almost certainly think of the Thoroughbred. The very name epitomizes its standing: it is taken from the Arabic word "Kehilan" meaning "pure bred." All Thoroughbreds, as is well known, trace their roots back to three Arabian sires, the "Darley Arabian," the "Godolphin Arabian," and the "Byerley Turk." Through these three fathers the purest blood lines were developed and some of the most famous racehorses have been produced; animals such as "Eclipse," born during a solar eclipse, who won 18 races with ease and went on to establish an important blood line. As time went on, less Arabian blood was infused into the breed. The English Thoroughbred is a superb racehorse and it also makes a good show jumper or event horse. Because of its qualities it has also long been used to improve other breeds. For example, many Thoroughbred lines have been established in the United States and Europe, each country having slightly different requirements for the horse.

Description: Any solid color is allowed, although the most commonly seen colors are chestnut, brown, or bay. In conformation the Thoroughbred has an intelligent head set on an elegant neck, very sloping shoulders, clean hard legs, a deep body, and a short back. Height can stand anywhere between 14.3 and 17 hands (4ft 9in and 5ft 8in).

WELSH COB

Origins: One of the best-loved and most striking of horses, the Welsh Cob is a superb exhibition horse. Believed to have originated during the 11th century, following cross-breeding of the stocky Welsh ponies with larger, imported horses, probably brought to the country by the Romans, the Welsh Cob was a prized warhorse. During the following few centuries, the popularity of the Welsh Cob declined, as more imports were brought back from travels and conquests abroad. Chief among these were the Arab horses acquired during the Crusades, together with the Andalusian and Barb breeds. Subsequent centuries saw a variety of cross-breeding experiments take place, most of which, rather than improving the breed, had the opposite effect. It is only during the later part of the 20th century that efforts have been made to preserve the breed. As well as their use as warhorses, which continued into this century, as the military found that they made ideal packhorses, Welsh Cobs have traditionally been used as farm animals or for light draft work. Today they are increasingly found in competitions such as jumping, cross-country, and driving.

Description: The Welsh Cob is a breed that possesses excellent stamina and energy, and has a gentle, friendly nature. It has a long and muscular neck, deep chest, and sturdy, well-muscled legs. The coat can be almost any color, and height stands at around 15 hands (5ft).

Holland

DUTCH DRAFT

Origins: Although the breed we recognize today was only officially registered in the early part of the 20th century, the breeding of large heavy draft horses had been taking place for many years before this. The breed came about due to demand for a heavy and powerful draft horse for agricultural use. Although still working, the increased mechanization of farms has made the breed less common today. Originally founded on crosses between Zeeland-type mares, Belgian Heavy Draft, and Belgian Ardennes stallions, since the early 20th century, breed purity has become very important and, since 1925, the stud book has been open only to hors-

es of recognized pedigree. It is prized as much for its placid temperament and steady pace as for its strength.

Description: Despite its size, the Dutch Draft has a certain agility, and is intelligent and tough. The head is well-proportioned on a short neck and the back is short and quite often hollow. The Dutch Draft has a deep chest, short, muscular legs, and very broad feet. The average height is around 16 hands (5ft 4in), and coat color is generally bay, chestnut, or gray. Black coats occur occasionally as well.

DUTCH WARMBLOOD

Origins: Most modern of the Dutch horse breeds, the Dutch Warmblood

was, like its Danish counterpart, founded during the 1960s. It was produced in response to a demand for athletic horses with speed and endurance that could also be used for competition work — primarily three-day events and show jumping. The base breeds were the Gelderland and Groningen, and this combination was then refined with further breeding to Thoroughbred stock. The result is a keen performance horse, exported all over the world. The governing body for the breed is the Dutch Warmblood Society, which oversees the breeding of the various types of Warmblood, whether they be for riding, competition events, or riding and driving. There are many famous Dutch Warmblood show jumpers, notably "Marius" and his equally famous son "Milton," and one of the best-known current dressage horses is Jennie Loriston-Clarke's "Dutch Courage." In 1980 a team of Dutch Warmbloods won the bronze at the World Carriage Driving Championships.

Description: The competition Warmblood has a Thoroughbred type of head, a shorter body than the Gelderland, and sound, strong, well-muscled limbs and body. It has a notably smooth and flowing gait, which enhances its competition performance. Any solid color is permissible and height stands at 15.3 hands to 16 hands (5ft 1in to 5ft 4in).

FRIESIAN

Origins: One of the oldest of the European breeds, the Friesian was used by the Roman legions and was used as a warhorse during the Middle Ages. Highly popular because of its willing and gentle nature, it was also put to use extensively for farm work as farmers could leave unskilled labor to handle the horse without mishaps. The Romans also took Friesian horses with them to Great Britain, where they had a great influence on the way that the Dales and Fell developed. Other breeds influenced by the Friesian were the Dole Gudbrandsdal, Clydesdale, and Shire. Friesian blood was also used to help develop breeds of trotting horses. Too much cross-breeding, however, corrupted the purity of the breed, and steps had to be taken to control breeding stock. To this end the Friesian stud book was founded in 1879. Before they can be entered in the stud book, mares and stallions have to meet high standards of pedigree and conformation. Farm mechanization caused a decline in numbers, except during World War II, when they were heavily in demand as working horses again. Today the Friesian is used as a carriage horse, and does well in competition work. Its color and appearance also made it a popular choice for undertakers!

Description: The Friesian is noted for its very high action fast trot, which makes it an ideal harness horse. The long alert head, carried on an arched neck, has short ears. Shoulders, back, and limbs are strong; the legs are feathered. Height stands between 15 hands and 15.3 hands (5ft and 5ft 1in). Friesian horses are always black, although a small white star is allowed. Another characteristic of the Friesian horse is an exceptionally long, thick mane and tail.

GELDERLANDER

Origins: Named for the Dutch province, the Gelderland is probably best known for being one of the foundation breeds of the Dutch Warmblood. It has its origins in a very old native breed that was crossed to other breeds such as the Norfolk Roadster, Holstein, and Oldenburg. Later breeding crosses were also made to Thoroughbreds and Arabians. This resulted in a distinctive horse with stylish action, a breed that has found a

FRIESIAN STALLION

home in several royal stud farms; Great Britain's included. The Gelderland was mainly used for light farm work, yet was also an outstanding carriage horse and heavyweight riding horse. Its elegant bearing, smooth gait, and attractive appearance mean that it is still a popular carriage horse today.

Description: In common with other Dutch horse breeds, the Gelderlander has a docile and willing nature. The head is large and plain, but softened with a kindly expression. The body is wide and deep with strong shoulders and the Gelderlander also has slim, well-proportioned yet muscular legs. Continued cross-breeding with the English Thoroughbred has produced horses that have played an important part in the recent development of the Dutch Warmblood breed. Usual color is chestnut, height stands at 15.2 to 16.2 hands (5ft 1in to 5ft 5in), although larger animals are sometimes found.

GRONINGEN

Origins: In essence an agricultural horse, the Groningen is the second breed that provided the foundation stock for the successful Dutch Warmblood, and comes from the Groningen region of Holland. Presently it is a light draft horse, but until fairly recently it was considerably heavier in action and shape, being based on the Friesian breed. Primarily a farm horse, it could also be used as a carriage horse though it lacked the pace of the Gelderlander. Later influences used to lighten the breed were the Oldenburg and Friesian. This has lead to a breed that is a fast and elegant carriage horse, possessing great stamina and considerable intelligence.

Description: The breed is well-known for its docile temperament and willingness to learn. The head is plain and the horse has a shortish neck and long body. Color is usually brown or bay. Height is between 15.2 hands and 16.2 hands (5ft 1in and 5ft 5in).

Hungary

GIDRAN

Origins: Also known as Hungarian Anglo-Arabian. The Gidran breed takes its name from its founding stallions. The first stallion, a chestnut Siglavy Arab called "Gidran Senior," was imported from the Middle East in 1816. His foal, "Gidran II," born in 1820 by a Spanish mare, is widely credited as being the father of the Gidran breed. Subsequent crosses, including English Thoroughbreds followed, producing the Gidran we know today, and accounts for its other recognized name of Hungarian Anglo-Arab. The original purpose of the Gidran was as a military horse though it has since been used for light draft work. It is more commonly known today as a riding and competition horse; particularly excellent for jumping. Gidran stallions are also popularly crossed with other horses to improve other breeds.

Description: The Gidran is courageous, fast, and energetic, making it a superb competitor. However, it has a somewhat unstable temperament and can be fiery. The Gidran's Arabian blood can be seen in its elegant bearing and fine features: it has a small head, a long, well-proportioned neck, a deep chest, and well-formed, muscular legs. Coat coloration is, almost without exception, chestnut. Gidran height stands between 16.1 and 17 hands (5ft 4in and 5ft 8in).

HUNGARIAN WARMBLOOD

Origins: Also known as Hungarian Sport Horse. The Hungarian Warmblood was developed through a selective breeding program at the Mezohegyes State Stud. The desire was to produce a good all-round sporting breed; one that would excel at all competitive sports. The breeding process involved crossing a selection of Hungarian horses, such as the Nonius, Kisber-Felver, and Gidran, with European warmblood breeds such as the Dutch Warmblood and the Holstein. The program was successful, and today's Hungarian Warmblood excels at all sports, from show jumping through dressage and driving events. Hungarian Warmbloods have had much success in international sporting events, with one horse, "Randi," winning Grand Prix events in five cities. Another horse, "Heritage Poker," has been equally successful in Volvo World Cup competitions.

Description: Today's Hungarian Warmblood is a more elegant horse than its forebears, and is famous for its attractive appearance, intelligence, good nature, and energy. Coat coloration can be any solid color, although brown tones are most common. Average height stands between 16 and 17 hands (5ft 4in and 5ft 8in).

KISBER FELVER

Origins: Also known as Hungarian Half-bred. The stallion, "Kisber," named for the stud on which he was bred, was the founder of the Kisber Felver breed. Using imported English Thoroughbreds, the aim of the Kisber stud was to produce a superior breed of race horses, an aim in which it was entirely successful. Indeed, the stallion "Kisber" himself was a Derby winner in 1876. The selective breeding

program employed by the stud has resulted in what is widely regarded as the most attractive and elegant racing breed in the world. Athletic, good-natured, and possessing excellent stamina, the Kisber Felber is an excellent event and competition horse. It has also been used to improve other breeds, such as a variety of the Trakehner breed, the Burnus, which owes more of its characteristics to the Kisber Felver than to its namesake. Unfortunately, the upheavals in Hungary following the two world wars has left the Kisber Felber in a sorry state, and there are not many pure-breds left today, although efforts are being made to preserve the breed.

Description: Today, the more popular Half-bred is that based on the Lipizzaner, rather than Thoroughbred stock. This is smaller, and has an excellent reputation as a superior driving horse. The Kisber Felver coloration encompasses most colors, and its average height ranges between 15.3 to 17 hands (5ft 1in to 5ft 8in).

NONIUS

Origins: The Nonius owes its name to a stallion foaled in France and taken to Hungary with a group of other Normandy horses. "Nonius's" sire was "Orion," an English half-bred, his dam a Norman mare. "Nonius" proved highly successful as a sire when put to the local mares, and also those with Arabian, Andalusian, Turkish, and Lipizzaner blood. Used extensively by the military and by farmers, as with many Hungarian horses of the 19th century, the Nonius proved highly popular and many were exported abroad as cavalry remounts. The latter half of the century saw the breed being influenced by more Thoroughbred blood, causing it to develop into two types. The most popular is the Large Nonius, which is heavier and taller, and heavily influenced by the English Thoroughbred. This type stands at 15.3 hands to 16.2 hands (5ft 1in to 5ft 5in). It was once used as a horse artillery wheeler, but is now mainly used for driving. The

second type is the Small Nonius, based on the Anglo-Norman, and not as attractive as its larger relative. This is a lighter riding horse of about 14.3 hands to 15.3 hands (4ft 9in to 5ft 1in).

Description: In general, the Nonius is a well-built horse with a gentle temperament. It has a somewhat long head and neck, a long, but often hollow, back, and a deep chest. Legs are muscular and quite slim and hooves are particularly tough. The usual colors are dark bay, brown, or black.

FURIOSO

Origins: The Furioso is a relative of the Nonius. The breed was developed in the 19th century, when two Thoroughbred English stallions, "Furioso" and "North Star," were imported into Hungary's world-famous Mezohegyes stud. There they were bred with Nonius mares and

founded their own bloodlines. "North Star" was the son of "Touchstone," a St Leger winner. After some years, the two bloodlines eventually merged, with the Furioso becoming the more dominant though the breed is still often referred to as the Furioso-North Star. Today, the breed is used as a riding and competition horse, although it is also a popular harness horse.

Description: The Furioso has a strong compact body, with a well proportioned head and neck, a long, straight back and muscular legs. The breed stands at between 15.1 hands and 16.2 hands (5ft 1in and 5ft 5in). All solid colors are permissible, although brown, bay, and black are common.

SHAGYA ARAB

Origins: As with all of the Hungarian breeds, the Shagya Arab takes its name from the foundation sire. In 1816, a decree stated that Oriental blood should be added to Hungarian breeds destined for military use, and in 1836, an Arab stallion of the "Shagya" name was imported from the Bedouins to the state-owned Stud of Babolna. The chief aim of the stud was to breed a special type of Arab with which to supply riding horses to the famous Hungarian Light Cavalry. Some Shagya stallions were also exported to Poland once the breed had become established. These proved to be of enormous help in refining Polish breeds. The Shagya Arabian made an excellent riding and cavalry horse, but it was also used as a harness and light farm horse. The modern-day Shagya Arabian makes a good competition horse.

Description: The original Shagya was tall for an Arabian at over 15 hands (5ft). Selective breeding has produced a breed of horse with the same shape and character of the original Arabian, but one that is bigger and broader. The Shagya Arabian has more bone and more correct hindlegs. It is also hardier and thrives on poor food. Height usually stands at 14.2 hands to 15 hands (4ft 8in to 5ft) and all solid colors are allowed, although the most usual color is gray.

SHAGYA ARAB

Iceland

ICELANDIC HORSE

Origins: Also known as the Iceland Tolter. The Icelandic Horse is not a native of Iceland, but was brought to the island by settlers during the 9th century. Its most likely ancestors include Danish and Norwegian horses, and European Celtic breeds. Since then, inbreeding and unsuccessful cross-breeding attempts have meant that the Icelandic breed has developed in relative purity. Since early days the Icelandic Horse has been used for all kinds of work, including riding, light draft, and agricultural. Iceland's harsh climate has also made these horses a valuable source of meat if other food supplies run scarce. Today their use has expanded, and they are widely exported outside Iceland. Their size makes them ideal mounts for children, and their hardiness and stamina also make them excellent trekking horses. For many years there was also a flourishing export trade to Britain, where they were used as pit ponies. Indeed, outside of Iceland, the horse is often classified as a pony.

Description: Icelandic Horses are prized for their independence, often being raised in half-wild conditions, foraging for themselves. They are sturdy, friendly, and versatile. Physically they are compact and have short, muscular necks, and short, stocky legs. The horse has a very distinctive gait, based on a three-beat, which provides an extremely comfortable ride. The most common color is chestnut, although other colors are also found. Average height stands between 13 and 14 hands (4ft 4in and 4ft 8in).

ICELANDIC HORSE

Iran

CASPIAN

Origins: For many years it was believed that the Caspian horse had been extinct for centuries. Then, in 1965, a small herd was discovered in the remote Elburz mountains, near the Caspian Sea by Mrs Louise Firouz, the American wife of an Iranian. Groups were eventually shipped to breeding centers around the world, with the aim of preserving this rare breed. Research has subsequently suggested that the Caspian is the direct descendent of an ancient Oriental horse, domesticated in Mesopotamia around 3000 BC. If,

as it appears, there has been no cross-breeding, the Caspian can surely claim to be one of the oldest and purest breeds in the world.

Description: Standing at between 10 and 12 hands (3ft 4in and 4ft), it has been argued that the Caspian is really a pony. However, the structure and characteristics of the Caspian clearly suggest that it is better classified as a true miniature horse breed. Well-proportioned, graceful, and sturdy, the Caspian has a muscular back and neck, short stocky legs, and a deep chest. It is friendly and intelligent,

making it an ideal riding horse, particularly suitable for children or beginners. Coat color is generally gray, bay, or chestnut.

PLATEAU PERSIAN

Origins: This breed name was created as recently as 1978, and was chosen by Iran's Royal Horse Society to encompass a number of Persian horse types, the most famous of which was the Persian Arab. Indeed, this name is still commonly used today. Persian horses are some of the oldest breeds in the world, and the Arab variety is believed to date back nearly 4,000 years. Other varieties from different regions have also been hugely influenced by the Arab bloodline. These include the Jaf, the Darashouri, and

Shirazis. All of these types have predominantly Arab ancestry, although with differing levels of miscellaneous blood from crosses over the years with other breeds.

Description: Persian horses are extremely attractive and, thanks to their Arab forebears, they have rather a noble bearing. Their native environment is dry and rocky, so they have adapted to their terrain by developing very hard feet and a somewhat stockier frame than the traditional light Arab build. These horses have been used for riding for many centuries, and possess speed and stamina, as well as energy and a degree of high-spirits. Coat coloration is usually chestnut, gray, or bay and height stands at around 15 hands (5ft).

Ireland

Irish Draft

Origins: More of a lightweight than a heavy draft horse, the Irish Draft makes an exceptional hunter. These horses are rumored to be descended from the Connemara, although no research has actually proved this. It seems possible that there is also some Clydesdale blood, the result of cross-breeding from imports that came to Ireland in the 19th century. The first stud book was opened in 1917, and in the following years many examples of this breed were sent to war, where they suffered heavy losses. Since the curbing of export to the Continent in the mid-1960s, the breed is beginning to flourish in greater numbers in its native Ireland. However, increased mechanization in the agricultural industry has meant that Irish Draft horses are less in demand than in previous generations, although some examples have been crossed with the Thoroughbred to produce show jumpers, known as Irish Hunters.

Description: The Irish Draft is a particularly well-proportioned horse, with a long back and deep chest. Legs are slim, solid, and muscular. Height stands between 15 hands and 1 7 hands (5ft and 5ft 8in). All solid colors are allowed, although gray, brown, and chestnut are most common.

IRISH DRAFT

Italy

ITALIAN HEAVY DRAFT

Origins: A relatively new breed, the Italian Heavy Draft was developed in 1860 at the Ferrera state stud. Original crosses were made with native horses and imported Arab, Thoroughbred, and Hackney stock. The result was not entirely satisfactory, and from the beginning of the 20th century, efforts were made to increase size, to produce a true heavy draft horse. Cross-breeding experiments with the Percheron, Brabant, and Boulonnais did not achieve the desired effect, which was a strong yet agile horse, of less bulk than its Heavy Draft counterparts. Eventually a cross was made with the Breton Postier, a much lighter horse. The result was a success, and forms the basis of today's horse.

Description: Smaller than average for its type, the Italian Heavy Draft is strong enough to cope well with its work as an agricultural and draft horse. Its speed has given rise to its Italian name of Quick Heavy Draft

SALERNO

(*Tiro Pesante Rapido*). Good natured and docile, the Italian Heavy Draft is reasonably hardy. Main characteristics include a short, broad neck, a broad, muscular chest, and short, well-muscled legs. Coat color is generally chestnut, although bay and roan are also common. Height stands at around 14.2 to 15.2 hands (4ft 9in-5ft 1in).

SALERNO

Origins: This breed originated in the Campania region of Italy. A descendent of the Neapolitan breed, prized during the Middle Ages, the Salerno used to be popular as a cavalry horse; it is now greatly reduced in numbers and is used for competition work and as a general riding horse. During the 18th century it was known as the Persano, after the stud farm founded by Charles III of Naples and the foundation horses were crossed with Andalusian and Neopolitan blood at that time. The stud closed when the Italian monarchy was abolished, but breeding was re-established during the early 1900s, and this time the Persano was known as the Salerno. It has found fame as a carriage horse and, recently, as a high-class riding horse.

Description: The Salerno is a good-looking horse, showing later Thoroughbred influences. It has a fine head on a long, graceful neck, with long, slim but powerful legs. Height stands at 15.3 hands to 16 hands (5ft 1in to 5ft 4in). All solid colors are permissible, with chestnut brown and bay being most popular. Gray, although at one time very common, is now extremely rare.

SARDINIAN

Origins: Also known as Sardinian Anglo-Arab. The Sardinian is based on crosses between native Sardinian mares and Arab stallions that took place during the Saracen occupation of the island many centuries ago. This was followed in the 16th century, when imported Spanish stallions also added to the mix, and improved the local breed greatly. The 18th century saw the decline of the Sardinian breed, and it was not until the beginning of the 20th century that breeders began to care for and improve the breed once more. A new infusion of Arab blood was introduced, followed by some cross-breeding with the English Thoroughbred. The resulting horse is a fine, relatively small, but tough and nimble animal. Generally used as a riding horse, it is suitable both as a pleasure mount and for sports. It jumps well, and has plenty of stamina as well as considerable speed.

Description: The Sardinian is one of the favored mounts for the police force, due to its even temper, agility

and intelligence. The Sardinian has an elegant carriage, with slim, but strong, legs and a thick neck. Chestnut is a common coat color, although almost all solid colors occur. Height stands at around 15 to 15.2 hands (5ft-5ft 1in).

MAREMMANA/MAREMMANO

Origins: A hardy, essentially wild breed of the Tuscan region of Italy, the Maremmana was used by the local cattle breeders to help herd their stock. It is a well-built and hardy animal, well able to endure harsh conditions and a long working day. The Maremmano is well-liked for its general versatility and because it is economical to keep. It is used for a number of purposes in Italy: as a farm horse, riding horse, police, and army mount. No one quite knows how it came to its present type, although in recent years there have been crossings with the English Thoroughbred. This has refined the appearance of the Maremmana, making it lighter in build and more elegant, but the resulting horse is not as hardy as its forebears.

Description: The Maremmana has a long, heavy head on a long, muscular neck. It has long legs, which are sturdy and well-muscled. Height stands at 15.3 hands (5ft 1in). All solid colors are allowed.

MURGESE

MURGESE

Origins: From the horse breeding area of Murge in Italy, the modern Murgese is a light draft and riding horse. Its origins can be traced back to the time of Spanish occupation. The Spanish invaders brought with them Barb and Arab horses, and these cross-bred with native horses to produce the ancestors of today's Murgese. Development of the modern breed began in the 1920s, and was based on two earlier types, one of which has died out.

Description: A strong horse and a good worker, Murgese mares are sometimes used to breed mules. The Murgese is characterized by a light head on a sturdy neck, long legs with prominent joints, and a full chest. The usual color is chestnut, but black is often seen. Height stands at 14.3 hands to 16 hands (4ft 9in to 5ft 4in).

Japan

KISO

Origins: An ancient Japanese breed, that has been utilized as a work horse for many centuries, the precise ancestry of the Kiso is not known, although it is believed to have its origins with Mongolian horses that once roamed the grasslands. Although used in agriculture and for transport, the primary use of the Kiso for many years was as a cavalry horse. During the early part of the 20th century, breeding with larger horses, imported from the West, was actively encouraged by the government. Indeed, so zealous were they in trying to create a larger Japanese breed that around the time of World War II, the government ordered the castration of all Kiso stallions. That the breed survives, albeit as a rarity, today, is due to one stallion that escaped castration due to its position as a Shinto holy animal. The progeny of this stallion, "Shinmei," and a Kiso mare, produced the last purebred Kiso. Progeny of this horse, and Kiso crosses, have produced the breed as it stands today.

Description: A pure Kiso is, like most Japanese breeds, relatively small.

KISO

Mexico

AZTECA

Origins: The first breed developed in Mexico, the Azteca gained official registry in 1982. Founded by Don Antonio Ariza at his ranch San Antonio, the breed was developed by crossing imported Andalusian stallions with Quarter Horse, or mixed Quarter Horse and Criollo mares. An elegant and graceful breed, the Azteca has proved extremely adaptable, responding well to training in many disciplines. They are ideal for performance riding such as jumping or as the mount of the bullfighter, and their good-nature and sure-footedness also makes them suited to pleasure riding.

Description: The Azteca has a neat, lean head on a well-formed neck, a long, straight back, and slim, muscular legs. The Azteca mane is particularly

AZTECA

beautiful. The Azteca stallion should stand between 14.2 to 15.3 hands, while a mare should measure between 14.1 and 15.2 hands (4ft 8in and 5ft 1in). There is no color regulation, although some variations, such as paint or Appaloosa are not permitted.

GALICEÑO

Origins: The Galiceño is a small horse descended from horses bred in the Galician region of Spain and the Portuguese Garrano. Introduced to the South American continent by the Spanish conquistadores during the 16th century, the Galiceño is believed to have been one of the first horses brought to Mexico by Cortes in 1519. The breed was little known outside Mexico for many years and was only introduced into the United States during the late 1950s. A hardy, strong, intelligent and attractive breed, the Galiceño is also gentle and docile. It has been used by generations of Mexicans as a family horse, equally well-suited for use as a child's riding horse, as for a working saddle or cutting horse. Its strength and stamina belie its small size.

Description: Despite argument that the Galiceño should be classified as a pony, its characteristics clearly suggest those of a small horse. The proportions of the Galiceño can look quite odd, as it has an average-sized head on a comparatively short neck and back, with a narrow chest. It also has long legs for its size. Standing around 12.2 to 13.2 hands (4ft 1in to 4ft 5in), accepted breed coloration includes all solid colors, while albino and pinto markings are not allowed.

Morocco

BARB

Origins: A horse native to Morocco and Algeria, the Barb is an ancient breed that may be descended from a group of wild horses that escaped the Ice Age. Few other breeds have had as great an influence on horse bloodlines than the Barb: the Thoroughbred in particular owes much of its development to this breed. Introduced into parts of Europe during the 8th century following the invasion of Spain by the Moors, the Barb was one of the founders of the Andalusian breed. Examples were then imported into Great Britain during the 17th and 18th centuries and were used to help create the Thoroughbred racehorse. However, after a while its popularity in Britain began to decline, probably because it could not compete with the Arabian. In its homeland the Barb is held in high esteem by Berber tribesmen who called it the "Drinker of the Wind."

Description: Although it is highly likely that the Barb has at sometime been cross-bred with the Arabian, there are still great differences between the two breeds. The Barb has a longer, and much more primitive head and more sloping hindquarters than the Arab. All solid colors are allowed; height stands at 14 hands to 15 hands (4ft 8in to 5ft).

Norway

Dole Gudbrandsdal

Origins: Originally found in the Gudbrandsdal valley in the center of Norway, hence the breed name, the Dole is similar in looks to the British Fell and Dales ponies, which may be due to Friesian blood being present in all three breeds. There are different types of Dole, although all are noted for their trotting ability. Some are heavily built and best used as draft horses — the Dole Gudbrandsdals. A lighter version, known as the Dole Trotter, is used for harness racing. The Trotter was heavily influenced by a Thoroughbred stallion imported to Norway in 1834. Another much earlier influence on the breed was a now extinct cold-blooded type of heavy horse. The Dole is also well known in Poland and Sweden.

Description: The Dole is not overly tall, standing at between 14.2 hands and 15.2 hands (4ft 9in and 5ft 1in). It is, however, extremely powerful, with a strong body and muscular hind quarters. The Dole has a heavy head, short, well-muscled neck and a long back. Its legs are short but well-muscled, and the feet are broad and tough. The heavier version is noted for having more feather on the legs.

DOLE

Peru

PERUVIAN PASO

Origins: Also known as the Peruvian Stepping Horse. Sharing the Spanish ancestry of the Paso Fino, dating back to the 16th century conquistadores, the Peruvian Paso is also a horse well-known for its rhythmic gaits, but has developed under different conditions and for different purposes. Bred predominantly at high altitudes, the Peruvian Paso is hardy and possesses great stamina. It is capable of travelling for long distances over harsh, rocky mountains and carrying either packs or a rider. The flowing gait of the Peruvian Paso means that a rider will receive a comfortable ride, no matter how far the journey, and also means that the horse can travel long distances without getting tired. As well as this special gait, the Peruvian Paso is also exceptionally nimble, able to negotiate steep slopes, slippery ground and sliding rocks without fear or difficulty. Unlike many of today's breeds, the Peruvian Paso has maintained its purity over several centuries, with no outside blood being introduced.

Description: An excellent show horse, the Peruvian Paso is gentle, energetic and intelligent, attributes that also suit its alternative uses as a riding and ranching horse. Coat color is most commonly chestnut or bay, although almost all solid colors occur. The average height of a Peruvian Paso is from 14 to 15 hands (4ft 8in to 5ft).

PERUVIAN PASO

Puerto Rico

PASO FINO

Origins: Like so many of the South American breeds, The Paso Fino can trace its ancestry back to the Spanish horses brought to the Americas by the conquistadores in the 16th century. It is closely related to the Peruvian Paso, or Peruvian Stepping Horse which shares its history, but it possesses considerably different characteristics due to the difference in the conditions and environment in which it was bred. Developed both for transportation and as a show horse, the Paso Fino takes its name from the slowest of the four-beat gaits for which it is famous; the others being the fast paso largo and the smooth paso corto. Surprisingly, the Paso Fino does not have to be taught these movements they are entirely natural to the breed.

Description: A natural show-horse, the Paso Fino is extremely intelligent, gentle, energetic, and elegant. It has a well-proportioned build, with a strong, muscular neck, short back, and strong legs. It is very easy to train, and as well as being a superb performance horse, the Paso Fino is at home as a light working horse, such as drawing a carriage, ranching, as a riding horse, or racing horse. Almost any color and pattern is allowed and height stands from 14.2 to 15 hands (4ft 9in to 5ft).

PASO FINO

108

Poland

MALAPOLSKI

Origins: Also known as Polish Anglo-Arab. Developed by the Poles primarily as a sports riding horse, the Malapolski shares its origins with another Polish breed, the Wielkopolski, although today the two breeds are very different. Initial crosses were made with local stock and using both Arab and Thoroughbred horses. Later crosses were made with two Hungarian breeds: the Furioso and the Gidran. These later crosses have resulted in two distinct types of Malapolski. One, the Darbowsko-Tarnowski, has been strongly influenced by the Gidran. The other, the Sadecki, owes its characteristics and appearance more to the Furioso. The Malapolski is a strong and good-natured horse, quick to learn and high-spirited, although without being highly-strung. It performs well in competition, particularly jumping, and its equable temperament also makes it a fine pleasure riding horse. Its strength and stamina also make it suitable for light draft use such as carriage work.

Description: With fine features, including long legs, long neck, and

110

WIELKAPOLSKI

back, the Arab ancestry of the Malapolski can be plainly identified. The Malapolski coat can include most solid colors, although gray, black, chestnut, and bay are common. Height stands at around 15.3 to 16.2 hands (5ft 1in to 5ft 5in).

WIELKOPOLSKI

Origins: The Wielkopolski is a combination of two Polish breeds, the Poznan and the Masuren, which each possessed a considerable proportion of Arab, English Thoroughbred, and Hanoverian blood. Subsequently, both breeds also had a great deal of Trakehner blood after the Poles gained control of the Prussian Trakehnen stud and amalgamated the remaining bloodstock. The Wielkopolski has many uses: heavier examples can be used for light farm work, while lighter animals are suited for use in harness, riding, and competition events. There are now several Polish state studs, some of which specially breed the Wielkopolski for eventing.

Description: These horses are noted for their temperament and powerful conformation. They have well-proportioned heads and necks, with the neck being slightly arched. The back and the legs are quite long and the chest deep. Height is 16 to 16.2 hands (5ft 4in to 5ft 6in). All solid colors are permitted though chestnut is common.

Portugal

ALTER-REAL

Origins: To keep up with the fashion for court Haute êcole demonstrations in the 18th century, the Portuguese started their own royal stud. This resulted in the importation of several hundred Andalusian mares from Spain in 1747. From these mares, the Alter breed was founded. The resulting horses were noble looking and intelligent, well suited to Haute êcole work but the stud was overrun by Napoleon's troops and shortly after was disbanded. The Alter breed was nearly destroyed following attempts at breeding with Thoroughbred, Arab, and Hanoverian horses. Fortunately, the breed was rescued when Andalusian horses were once more imported, enabling the breed to return almost to its original state. These modern attempts to reintroduce the breed were begun in the 1930s, when the Portuguese Ministry of Economy took over the breed's welfare.

Description: The Alter-Real has a well-proportioned head on a somewhat short neck, a short back, and a

SORRAIA: PORTUGAL

broad, deep chest. The legs are well-built, slim, and muscular. The modern Alter-Real stands at between 15 and 16 hands (5ft and 5ft 4in); the usual colors are gray, brown, or bay.

LUSITANO

Origins: The Portuguese have their own version of the Spanish Andalusian: the Lusitano. This horse probably has similar ancestry to the Andalusian, although its exact history is uncertain. Agile and athletic, well suited to the movements of Haute êcole, the Lusitano is the favorite of mounted bullfighters and is often used in demonstrations. It was also a favorite of the Portuguese cavalry, as well as being an excellent carriage horse. With the popularity of bullfights in decline due to worldwide disapprobation, the Lusitano, although still the top breed in Portugal, is no longer as popular as it once was. In fact, the Lusitano is now better known outside Portugal, especially in the US.

Description: The Lusitano is very similar to the Andalusian in general appearance, with the same small, convex-shaped head, thick neck, solid legs, short, straight back, and the same characteristic full mane and tail. Usual colors for the Lusitano are brown and black, and average height stands at 15 to 16 hands (5ft to 5ft 4in).

SORRAIA

Origins: A descendent of the original wild horses that roamed throughout Spain and Portugal for centuries, the breed was named for the Sorraia river lowlands where they were discovered living wild at the beginning of the 20th century. The breed can still be found wild in Portugal, and some are also believed to exist among the wild horse herds of the United States, where they

ALTER REAL

are similar to the Mustang. The Sorraia is believed to have contributed to the development of Spanish breeds such as the Andalusian and the Lusitano. As these have influenced many subsequent breeds themselves, the importance of the Sorraia in equine history is considerable.

Description: The appearance of the Sorraia would suggest some Asiatic blood in its make-up. However, it seems that little cross-breeding has taken place, so the Sorraia we see today may look no different from its ancestors. The Sorraia has a short head and the ears are black-tipped, its chest is rather lean and it has relatively long legs. Coat color is nearly always dun, often with some striped markings. A rather small horse, standing at around 14.1 hands (4ft 8in), the Sorraia is often mistakenly classified as a pony, although research suggests it more readily conforms to horse type.

Spain

ANDALUSIAN

Origins: Many people believe that Spanish Iberian horses were crossed with the Barb to produce the Andalusian; others believe that the former breed had been extinct for thousands of years before this took place. Whether or not it is true, the Andalusian was one of the premier breeds of Europe, dominating horse breeding and culture from the 12th to 17th centuries. No important European court was complete without its own high school of horse performing Haute êcole, and the Andalusian was perfect for this work. Their blood is to be found in nearly all of the great breeds of horses, including the world famous Lipizzaner. The Andalusian was particularly important in the US. Examples of the breed were shipped to the States with the colonists. Many American breeds, such as the Appaloosa, were based on Andalusian horses. The Carthusian monks of Jerez de la Frontera, Seville, and Castille maintained lines of pure-bred Andalusians, when elsewhere cross-breeding was threatening the breed.

Description: The Andalusian is an athletic horse with high stepping paces and much presence. It has an elegant bearing, with a noble head on an arched neck. Its back is short, chest

ANDALUSIAN

deep, and the legs strong, slim, and well muscled. Height is about 15.2 hands (5ft 1in). The usual color is gray.

CARTHUSIAN

Origins: Also known as the Carthusian-Andalusia, or Carthujano. The Carthusian is one of the oldest and most prestigious of Spanish breeds. Founded on horses of pure Andalusian bloodline, the Carthusians take their name from the monks of Jerez de la Frontera, whose reputation as superior horse breeders can be traced back to the 15th century. Over the centuries the Carthusian monks guarded the bloodline of their horses zealously, and so determined were they that the breed should remain pure, they refused to obey the royal command to introduce Neapolitan blood to the breed. During the Peninsular Wars (1808-1814),

Napoleon stole a large proportion of the stock, but the few horses that remained were gathered by the monks, who continued to breed them. In the mid-18th century, a few select breeders purchased mares from the monks. These breeders shared the aim of the monks to maintain the pure Carthusian bloodline, and today these beautiful horses are still bred, primarily on state-owned studs.

Description: Standing at a maximum height of 15.2 hands (5ft 1in), Carthusians are generally gray, although chestnut and black coats can also be found. The head and neck are well-proportioned, with the neck being slightly arched. The legs are muscular and quite broad. A gentle, noble breed, the Carthusian today is generally used for both pleasure and performance riding, and occasionally for light draft work.

Sweden

NORTH SWEDISH

Origins: Often known as the North Swedish Trotter, the North Swedish horse shares much of its development with its Norwegian neighbor, the Dole. The North Swedish horse is a small draft horse, used extensively by the Swedish army as well as foresters. The lighter Trotter type has been developed by crossing the original horses with imported Trotter breeds, to produce a good trotting horse, but one that is far from overtaking the more famous Trotters.

Description: The breed has a large head with a short neck and strong shoulders. The quarters are strong and rounded with a sloping croup. These horses have a kindly temperament and are a long-lived breed. All solid colors are allowed; height stands at about 15.3 hands (5ft 1in).

SWEDISH WARMBLOOD

Origins: The Swedish Warmblood was developed from local stock crossed with warm-blooded breeds such as the Hanoverian, Thoroughbred, and Trakehner. Today the Swedish

SWEDISH WARMBLOOD

Warmblood is a powerful competition horse, but it was originally bred to fulfil the Swedish army's need for cavalry remounts. Indeed, the Swedish government owns its own stud farm at Flyinge where breeding programs have been in place for over 300 years. A stud book was opened in 1874 and strict standards were set to qualify for entry. These days, stock must also undertake a number of tests, including riding and harness tests. Other important points are conformation, performance, veterinary history, and action. A full breeding license is only granted after examination of their first offspring after they reach three years old. Such rigorous attention to detail has worked well for the Swedes, as the Swedish Warmblood is in great demand not only for the ridden disciplines, but also harness events.

Description: The head is well-proportioned, with big, bold eyes and an alert expression. Shoulders are strong, the body is compact and well-muscled with plenty of girth. Limbs are short and strong. Height is between 15.2 and 16.2 hands (5ft 1in and 5ft 5in).

Switzerland

SWISS WARMBLOOD

Origins: Also known as Swiss Halfbred or Einsiedler. Based on the old Swiss breed, the Einsiedler, and still recognized by that name today, the Swiss Warmblood is believed to have originated in Switzerland during the 11th century on a stud run by Benedictine monks, who were renowned for their horse breeding skills at this time. As the centuries progressed, a program of cross-breeding was introduced, with Norman and Hackney blood producing fine results. During the 20th century, Selle Français and French Anglo-Arab blood was used, and more recently crosses have taken place using Thoroughbred, Swedish, and German

SWISS WARMBLOOD MARE & FOAL

stock. This refined breeding produced the horse known today as the Swiss Warmblood, an attractive and elegant horse, predominantly used for riding and in competitions, where it excels in show jumping and dressage events. Swiss Warmbloods are also used for light draft work such as drawing carriages.

Description: These horses have deep chests and straight backs, with strong, well-defined and muscular legs. The body is powerful. Its superior appearance is matched by a temperament that is amenable, easily trained, and docile. Swiss Warmbloods stand at around 15.1 to 16.2 hands (5ft to 5ft 4in), and their coats can be any solid color, with brown the most common.

United States of America

AMERICAN CREAM DRAFT

Origins: The first recorded American Cream, "Old Granny" made her appearance in Iowa in 1911. Her colts had a particularly striking appearance, and one, "Nelson's Buck," was retained for breeding, giving rise to a new draft breed, characterized by its rich cream color, pink skin, amber eyes, and white mane and tail. "Old Granny" and subsequent mares were mated with draft bloodlines such as Belgians and Percherons, culminating

Hudson Thompson of Nebraska, who purchased the pink-skinned, pure white stallion "Old King" in 1917, the American Creme and White breed was successfully achieved through selective breeding with Morgan mares. Known as the American Albino horse, the breed flourished under the care of Caleb and his wife Ruth. Their tours of North America and Canada as the White Horse Troupe made their breed famous. In 1937 Caleb and Ruth founded the American Albino Horse Club (AAHC) to record "Old King's" progeny. Eventually this expanded to incorporate horses of the same coloration, but from different bloodlines, and so the American Albino became a true color breed. Over the years the AAHC underwent several changes and expansions, and during the 70s the American Albino horse became the American White, and a further division included the American Creme.

in the influential stallion "Silver Lace," foaled in 1931. It was the interest in colts sired by "Silver Lace" that lead to the founding of the American Cream Horse Association of America in 1944. Recognized as a standard draft breed in 1950, blood tests subsequently concluded that the American Cream was truly a separate breed, and not simply a color breed as had been thought.

Description: The American Cream has a placid and adaptable disposition and is easily trained, making it ideally suited for hitching and driving. A hard-working breed, it is classified as a medium-heavy draft horse. A mature mare can weigh around 1,700 to 1,800 pounds, while a stallion can top the scales at one ton. Height is around 15 to 16.3 hands (5ft to 5ft 5in).

AMERICAN CREME AND WHITE

Origins: Also known as American Albino. Founded by Caleb and

Description: A versatile breed, the Creme and White is suitable for most types of use. Although their pale skin makes them prone to sun-sensitivity, they do not suffer from complaints typically associated with albinos, such as blindness or deafness. Both American Whites and Cremes must have pink skin. A true White must also have a pure white coat, while the coat of a Creme can range from pale ivory to cream. Eye color is not restricted. Height is from 14 to 16 hands (4ft 8in to 5ft 4in), depending on bloodline.

AMERICAN MINIATURE

Origins: Acceptance into the American Miniature breed is strictly determined by height. To be allowed, the maximum height from the ground to the withers for a full-grown Miniature must be no more than 34 inches. This small height is the principle characteristic of the breed, and other aspects of a particular horse's appearance may vary, depending on which full-sized horse breed it is based on. Most Miniatures look somewhat like "toy" versions of their larger relatives, which can include Thoroughbreds, Arabs, and Quarter Horses. American Miniature Horses are strictly regulated by their Association, who are quick to point out that miniatures are not genetic anomalies or "freaks." Rather, these small horses share the conformation and proportions of larger breeds simply reduced in scale. The Miniature is prized as a show horse, and competition between owners can be fierce.

Description: Miniature Horses possess gentle natures and a high degree of intelligence, which, coupled with their diminutive size, makes them perfect pets, and ideal companions for children. Their needs in terms of space and feed is similarly reduced, making them reasonably inexpensive to keep and maintain. Almost all colors and patterns can be found within the American Miniature breed.

APPALOOSA

Origins: An American saddle horse, the breed can be traced back to horses found in central Idaho and may have originally been bred as a warhorse. The name Appaloosa is a corruption of "Palouse," the river within the region where the horse was originally located. Its origins go back to the horses brought by the Spanish conquistadores during the 16th century. It was a Native American Indian tribe, the Nez Perce, who crossed the horse to produce the distinctive characteristics we know today.

Description: The Appaloosa is best known for its spotted coat, which may be all-over spotted, loins and quarters

only spotted or light spots on a dark background (leopard). However, these markings only appear as a horse matures — foals are born with plain coats. The Appaloosa is known as a riding horse and, because of its unusual and rather glamorous looks, is often used in parades and circuses. The Appaloosa ranges from 14.2 to 15.2 hands (4ft 9in to 5ft 1in). The breed has good strong shoulders and strong legs with plenty of bone. Arabian influences have also given the horse an attractive head and good carriage.

AMERICAN SADDLEBRED

Origins: The modern Saddlebred was founded in Kentucky and was at first called the Kentucky Saddler. The requirements of the breed's founders were that the horse should be smooth enough in action to ride around farms as well as being able to race and look good in harness. Influences were the Narragansett Pacer, Morgans, Hackneys, and Thoroughbreds. The "American Horse" has played an important part in its country's history, first being mentioned in government documents in 1776. Paul Revere is believed to have made his famous ride on a Narraganset Pacer. American Horses also featured as prized mounts in the War of Independence, as well as being favored by later pioneers, such as Daniel Boone. However, the breed that we know today as the American Saddlebred became famous during the Civil War, as three of the famous generals, Sherman, Lee, and Grant, chose Saddlebreds as their mounts.

Description: Three-gaited and five-gaited horses have several eye-catching paces: including the spectacular rack. The modern American Saddlebred makes a superb show

horse, and consequently is often used in parades and demonstrations. Height stands at 15 to 16 hands (5ft to 5ft 4in). All solid colors are allowed.

BUCKSKIN

Origins: Recent research has shown that the Buckskin, or Dun, can trace its development as far back as the earliest records. Studies of Buckskin origins suggest that the Buckskin ancestors may well be the Spanish Sorraia breed, whose blood can be found in many breeds all around the world.

Description: That the Buckskin is a true breed is evidenced by the many characteristics it has that are not typical of other breeds. Their bones and feet are especially tough and they are very hardy, able to cope with rough terrain and harsh climates. Buckskin color is light in hue, ranging from the golden coat of the stallion to a paler color usually found on mares. Some markings may be seen on the coat — these are often slightly reddish.

COLORADO RANGER

Origins: The Colorado Ranger has often been mistaken for a type of Appaloosa. However, although its appearance can be similar to the Appaloosa, it is a distinct breed in its own right. It is descended from the progeny of two horses — a Barb and an Arab — that the Sultan of Turkey gave as gifts to General Grant in 1878. The breed was developed by Mike Ruby, who, in 1934, was invited to exhibit a pair of his stallions by the National Western Stock Show Commission. The horses were very successful, and the breed was official-ly named as the Colorado Ranger that same year. Mike Ruby founded the Colorado Ranger Horse Association in 1935, and today the Association is still going strong, with annual exhibitions, shows, and performances.

Description: The Colorado Ranger shares the spotted appearance of the Appaloosa, as well as its varieties of colors and patterns. It is a strong, compact horse, used primarily as a saddle horse. It is well-proportioned with powerful limbs and a sturdy build. Its even temperament also makes it an excellent performance horse. Height stands around 15.2 hands (5ft 1in).

FLORIDA CRACKER

Origins: As with so many American horse breeds, the Florida Cracker has Spanish origins. The 16th and 17th centuries saw intensive exploration and colonization of the New World by the Spanish. These wanderers brought with them crops and livestock from their native country, and these Spanish horses flourished, both under the breeding programs begun by these early settlers, and in the wild, where escaped horses formed new herds that populated much of Florida for many years. These wild horses quickly adapted to the harsh Florida climate and terrain, and their hardiness and adaptability made them attractive to both the Native Americans, as well as the early pioneers, who soon began to use them as sturdy work horses. Primarily used to work cattle, the Florida Cracker became a good all-round worker, equally efficient as a farm horse, or hauling a wagon or carriage. The Florida Cracker takes its name from the Cracker people, who populated Florida in its early days. These people, in turn, got their name from the sharp crack of the whips they used to herd and round up their cattle.

Description: A Florida Cracker Horse can be almost any color. Solid colors are most common, however, with brown and gray being typical. A Cracker Horse stands between 13.2 to 15 hands (4ft 5in to 5ft) in height.

COLORADO RANGER

KIGER MUSTANG

Origins: The Kiger Mustang is believed to be the purest Mustang breed in the world today. More common Mustang breeds have had their Spanish blood diluted through crossbreeding over the years, but the Kiger Mustang still shows many of the characteristics of its Spanish, predominantly Barb, ancestry. This pure Mustang breed was discovered in a remote region of Oregon in 1977, with several groups being brought to breeders' attention. There was an immediate desire to foster and preserve the breed, which was subsequently split into two breeding groups. To maintain purity, care was taken that no other horses were in the vicinity of the Kiger herds.

Description: The Kiger Mustang shares many of the characteristics of other Mustang breeds, in that it is tough, hardy, and fiercely independent. Their build, as with other Mustangs, is quite coarse and heavy. It has a broad, muscular neck, a short back, and strong, stocky legs. Kiger Mustang coloration is dun, in various shades, with hardly any white markings. As with ordinary Mustangs, the average height of the Kiger Mustang is around 14 to 15 hands (4ft 8in to 5ft).

MISSOURI FOXTROTTER

Origins: Another of the American gaited breeds, the Missouri Foxtrotter originated in the Ozark mountains during the 19th century. Settlers of the area needed a mount that could be used to cover long distances comfortably: as a result the Missouri Foxtrotter gives one of the most comfortable of rides. The ambling four-beat gait needed to accomplish this became known as the foxtrot — the horse walks with

its front legs, but trots with its hind legs. At the same time, the horse moves its head in time to the rhythm of its hooves. This gait enables the Foxtrotter to proceed at speeds of up to eight miles per hour.

Description: The Foxtrotter is noted for its gentle nature and this, together with the speeds it can achieve and the long distances it can travel, makes it very popular today for trail riding. It has great stamina and energy, and is a hardy horse. Well-proportioned, the body of the Fox Trotter is wide and it has a short back and muscular hind legs. Height stands between 15 and 17 hands (5ft and 5ft 8in). All colors are allowed, but many are chestnut.

MORGAN

Origins: The Morgan must be one of the most famous and best-loved of American horses. One of the smaller US breeds, the Morgan can trace its beginnings back to just one stallion a little bay named "Justin Morgan" after his owner. Little is known of the horse's origins: he may well have had Arabian or Barb blood, while others suggest that he was sired by a Welsh Cob. "Justin Morgan" was famed for his ability to pull great weights and win races. Luckily, his owner decided to try him out as a stud horse before having him gelded. Whatever mare he was put to, the resulting foal always took after the sire. Demand for his services grew and he was eventually bought by the US Army. A Morgan Stud farm was founded in Woodstock Vermont, and the Morgan has also played a great part in the development of the American Standardbred. "Justin Morgan" lived on into his 20s.

Description: The Morgan is a popular all-rounder with a kindly and tractable nature. It has a well-proportioned

127

head, neck, and body, with excellent bone structure, giving the Morgan an extremely pleasing appearance. Although robust, its maximum height stands between 14 and 15.2 hands (4ft 8in and 5ft 1in) making it an ideal mount for either a child or an adult.

MUSTANG

Origins: Initially the term Mustang or Bronco was given to the semi-wild horses that roamed the plains of America, based on the horses imported by the Spanish in the 16th century. Inevitably, some of the conquistadores' horses escaped and bred in the wild; many were then captured by Native Americans. Original Mustangs showed their Spanish origins and were fine examples. However, as the breed grew wilder, and more cross-breedings occurred with escaped or wild horses of different breeds, its quality degenerated and although the animals were noted for their toughness, they grew scraggy in appearance. During the 20th century many Mustangs were shot because they were thought to be a nuisance to cattle. The breed is now protected, and efforts are being made to increase the numbers of the original "Spanish" Mustangs; those animals with obvious Barb origins. However, it is the more common, mixed-breed Mustang that holds the strongest place in the hearts of most Americans.

Description: These somewhat coarse-featured wild horses seem to represent the very essence of the "Old West." All colors are allowed, height ranges from 13.2 to 15 hands (4ft 5in to 5ft).

NATIONAL SHOW HORSE

Origins: Horse shows and other equestrian events are important industries in many parts of the world, particularly in the United States,

where increasing demand for the "perfect" show horse lead to the founding of the National Show Horse breed as recently as 1981. The breed was developed under the aegis of the National Show Horse Registry (NHSR), specially formed for the purpose by Gene La Croix. The aim of the NHSR was to produce a horse that was both beautiful, and athletic. The next step was to determine which current breeds exhibited these characteristics to the highest degree. Eventually the choice was made: the Arabian breed was chosen for its noble bearing, grace, and beauty, and its partner would be the American Saddlebred, which possessed both size and a fine stepping motion. Over the years, various combinations have been made always using these same two bloodlines.

Description: Today's animal is a strikingly attractive, energetic, proud, and intelligent animal, which has proved hugely popular in the show ring, and is credited with bringing in a new, wider audience. Characteristics of the National Show Horse depend on which bloodline is dominant. An Arab-based horse will stand at 14 to 15 hands (4ft 8in to 5ft), with coat color being generally black, chestnut, or brown. Horses with mainly American Saddlebred blood will be 15 to 16 hands (5ft to 5ft 4in), with a black, chestnut, gray, or bay coat.

PAINT HORSE

Origins: The Paint Horse is often classified as simply being a different name for the Pinto. However, the two breeds are clearly differentiated. Where the Pinto breed is based purely on color, and any bloodline can be accepted into the registry, acceptance as a member of the Paint breed also depends on accepted pedigree, with parentage registered with either the American Paint Horse Association, the American Quarter Horse Association, or the Jockey Club. The ancestors of today's Paint Horses were the wild horses that once roamed the central plains of the United States in their thousands. These were the descendants of the horses introduced into the New World by the conquistadores and settlers who began exploring the Americas in the 16th century. Inevitably, a large proportion of these wild horses were captured and tamed, first by the Native Americans, and later by cowboys and early pioneers, both attracted by the Paint's colorful markings. Today, the breed is extremely adaptable, at home in the show ring, on the ranch, and as a riding horse, both for pleasure and racing.

PAINT HORSES

Description: The Paint Horse is intelligent, stocky, and very powerful for its size. Its most distinctive characteristic is a patterned coat that features a solid color background, generally chestnut or bay, with white markings. Patterns fall into three main types. The Tobiano pattern is a usually solid color head, white legs, and large, regular, rounded flank markings. The Overo pattern has smaller, irregular spots, with white markings on the head but not on the lower back. The final pattern, Tovero, combines Tobiano and Overo markings. Height stands between 15.3 and 16.3 hands (5ft 1in and 5ft 5in).

Palomino

Origins: There have been gold Palomino horses since the time of the Ancient Greeks, although the name is later and could either come from a golden grape variety or Juan de Palomino. Horses of this color were sought after in Spain, particularly as Queen Isabella, sponsor of Columbus, favored them. The Spanish were responsible for introducing the color type into the US, which was one of the first countries to establish a breed society: the American Palomino Horse Association sets the standard by which a Palomino can be registered. To be accepted, one parent must either be Arabian, Thoroughbred, or Quarter Horse, and the other already registered. Today, the Palomino is popular as a saddle and show horse but they are also seen in Quarter Horse racing.

Description: Palomino identifies a color rather than a true breed. To qualify the coat must be the color of a newly minted gold coin, or three shades lighter or darker. The eyes must

have dark coloring. A Palomino will generally have a small head, long neck, and sloping shoulders. Legs are slim and well-muscled, and the whole body is well-proportioned. Height should be over 14 hands (4ft 8in).

PINTO

Origins: The Pinto has its origins in the Spanish horses brought to America during the 16th century. Many of these Spanish horses were eventually captured by Native American raiding parties, and cross-bred with native ponies to produce the highly characteristic Pinto breed.The eye-catching Pinto, or Painted Horse of America, is divided into two color types. The Ovaro has white patches starting from the belly, and coloring is usually dark. The Tobiano's white patches start elsewhere, usually from the back. A Pinto horse can be registered with two regis-

ters in the US: the American Paint Horse Association and the Pinto Horse Association.

Description: The Pinto is a color type rather than a breed, but there are certain points such as sound limbs and hard feet that are preferable. To be registered as a true Pinto, a horse must have one parent already registered, while the other parent must belong to either the Quarter Horse or English Thoroughbred breed. There are no height limits.

QUARTER HORSE

Origins: Founded on English and Spanish horses selectively bred by the first New World settlers during the 17th century, the American Quarter Horse is now the most numerous of the American breeds. The breed began life as a racehorse, which is how it got its name. Early racetracks in America usually had to be cleared specially for racing and the usual race distance was a quarter mile — thus the name Quarter Horse. Further developed by crossing Mustang and Thoroughbred blood, in addition to sprinting quarter-mile racetracks, the breed made a useful cattle horse. Quarter Horses are also now used for hunting, jumping, and as a polo mount.

Description: The Quarter Horse is noted for having an easy temperament and great acceleration. The head is short and wide, on a slightly arched neck. The back is short and straight and the legs muscular, particularly the thighs. The hindquarters are exceptionally powerful. This very popular horse has a large following outside the United States as well. All solid colors are allowed. Height stands at 15 to 16 hands (5ft to 5ft 4in).

Racking Horse

Origins: The Racking Horse has been popular in the United States for over 100 years. It was originally found primarily in the southern states, and its ancestry can be traced back to the early Walking Horses. Prized for its rhythmic, natural gait, the Racking Horse possessed the stamina to travel long distances, its smooth step allowing the rider to make the journey in considerable comfort. For many years the Racking Horse had no official recognition, registry, or breed name. It was simply a horse that featured in shows, but which did not belong to any particular type. However, during the 1960s a group of enthusiasts decided to try and obtain official recognition for the Racking Horse as a breed with very distinct characteristics. In 1971 they were successful, with breed recognition being gained and a registry founded. The name of

the breed, Racking Horse, was chosen as the single-footed gait of the horse was often referred to as "the rack."

Description: Breed qualification is largely based on possession of the natural gait. Strong and agile, good-natured and friendly, the Racking Horse is now a firm favorite throughout the United States. Coat color is primarily brown or bay, although other solid colors occur. The average height for a Racking Horse is around 15 hands (5ft).

Rocky Mountain Horse

Origins: The development of the Rocky Mountain Horse is largely due to one man, Sam Tuttle, who ran a riding stable in Kentucky, and who often hired horses to visitors eager to experience riding in the Appalachians. His most popular horse was the stallion, "Old Tobe," whose forebear was the Mustang, a breed descended from a mix of Spanish imports and native stock. "Old Tobe's" popularity was due to his agility, gentleness, and sure-footedness, making him ideally suited for even the most nervous of riders. Carefully fostered by Sam Tuttle, "Old Tobe's" progeny exhibited all their sire's characteristics, and so the Rocky Mountain Horse was created. Although a recent breed, The Rocky Mountain Horse is already extremely popular. A versatile riding horse, with great stamina, it is suitable for use in a wide variety of terrains, and its attractive appearance and gentle nature also make it a superb show horse. It is also used as a ranch horse.

Description: Today the breed is characterized by its smooth four beat gait, long neck, and wide chest. One of its most striking characteristics however is its color, which is an unusual chocolate brown. Height generally stands

QUARTER HORSE

ROCKY MOUNTAIN HORSE

133

around 14.3 hands (4ft 9in).

SPANISH BARB

Origins: When the Moors invaded Spain in the early 8th century, they brought their African-bred horses with them — the famous Barb. Mixing and breeding with indigenous breeds, the Barb was the forebear of many Spanish and Iberian horses, such as the Andalusian and the Jennet. These horses in turn accompanied the Spanish settlers during their exploration of the Americas in the 16th century. The Spanish Barb developed from these horses and became common within many of the southern states, where Spanish settlement was heaviest. It proved a popular horse with early cowboys and eventually formed the basis of several American breeds including both the Mustang and the Quarter Horse. The Spanish

Barb exists as a distinct breed today thanks to a few small breeding concerns, who have kept the bloodline pure. Official recognition of the breed only came about in the early 1970s.

Description: Prized for the smoothness of their gait and their endurance, which makes them ideal distance riding and ranching horses, the Spanish Barb is intelligent and quick to learn. Its temperament is generally even, although it is prone to high spirits. Coat coloration can include most solid colors, and the average height of a Spanish Barb stands between 13.2 and 14.1 hands (4ft 5in and 4ft 8in).

SPANISH MUSTANG

Origins: The Mustang is one of the most familiar and popular American breeds. Yet there are several distinct breed variations, which depend on specific bloodlines. The common Mustang is something of a mongrel breed, with ancestry that can be traced back to a wide variety of breeds. The Spanish Mustang, however, is of a purer type; the true descendent of the early horses formed from alliances between native ponies and imported Spanish breeds several centuries ago. Efforts were first made to preserve the breed during the 1950s, when an organization was formed to select prime, pure examples of the Spanish Mustang for breeding purposes. This was not an easy task, as the newly named Spanish Mustang was rare then, and indeed remains uncommon to this day.

Description: Preserving many of the traits of their Spanish forebears, such as hardiness, stamina, and adaptability, the Spanish Mustang today is a tough animal, capable of enduring harsh conditions. Proud and indepen-

dent, the Spanish Mustang's heritage can be traced in its rather elegant and noble appearance, compared to the relatively rough appearance of the common Mustang. However, it shares with other Mustang breeds a generally dun coat color, and an average height standing at between 14 and 15 hands (4ft 8in and 5ft).

SPANISH-NORMAN

Origins: A recently developed breed, the Spanish-Norman today recreates the original medieval warhorses, and is produced by cross-breeding the Spanish Andalusian with the French Percheron. Exhaustive studies were carried out to determine which breeds were best suited to the formation of the Spanish-Norman and these showed that the original Norman horses owed much to a Spanish ancestry, while also providing a foundation for the Percheron. Today, the Spanish-

SPANISH MUSTANGS IN NEVADA

Norman is an acclaimed sports horse and it is capturing both the attention and enthusiasm of horse fans across America. Its versatility makes it suitable for many kinds of performance work including dressage, exhibitions, jumping, and driving.

Description: The Spanish Norman's heritage has given it a striking appearance, with the beauty and noble bearing of its Andalusian relatives, and the sheer size and structure of the Percheron. Its docile temperament and intelligence makes it a willing learner, and extremely easy to train. The most common coat color is gray, although black and bay examples are also found. The body is well-proportioned and muscular, with strong sturdy legs, and broad shoulders and neck. Height can range between 15.2 and 17 hands (5ft 1in and 5ft 8in).
STANDARDBRED

Origins: Harness racing is one of the primary horse sports in America and the Standardbred was developed solely to meet the demand for a good trotting horse. The breed was fathered by "Hambletonian," who was a direct descendant of the English Thoroughbred "Messenger," who was in turn the son of the Norfolk Trotter "Bellfounder." Officially the name Standardbred dates from 1879, when the American Trotting Register set a speed standard as an entry requirement. (Modern rules admit horses on blood rather than speed alone.) Standardbred horses race by either trotting conventionally or pacing using a lateral movement. It is worth noting that pacers are more popular in America.

Description: In appearance the Standardbred is heavier set than the Thoroughbred, with hindlegs set behind the horse, giving greater propulsion. Its speed generally comes in short bursts, and very fast movement can be achieved in this way. A medium, well-formed head is set on a long, muscular neck. The back is long and generally straight and the legs powerful and muscular, particularly the thighs. The usual colors are bay but other colors are also found. Height stands at 14 hands to 16 hands (4ft 8in to 5ft 4in).

TENNESSEE WALKING HORSE

Origins: A breed developed to meet the needs of American plantation owners, the Tennessee Walking Horse was also known as the Plantation Walking Horse. As with the Morgan, the breed was founded by one stallion, "Black Allan," whose background was Morgan and "Hambletonian." "Black Allan's" son, "Roan Allan," with subsequent crosses with Standardbred and Saddlebred stock, resulted in the breed that we know today. The Walking Horse is famous for its unusual four-beat gaits: the flat walk, running walk, and the rocking chair canter. Although unusual, these gaits are completely natural. Show horses, however, are often shod with heavyweight shoes to enhance and show off their paces. The Tennessee Walking Horse Breeders' Association was founded in 1935.

Description: Together with many American breeds, the Tennessee Walking Horse is known for having a docile temperament. It has a large head on an arched neck, a straight, short back, and well-formed, muscular legs. All solid colors are permitted. Height stands at between 15 and 16 hands (5ft and 5ft 4in).

TENNESSEE WALKING HORSE

The Former USSR

AKHAL-TEKE

Origins: The Akhal-Teke is one of the world's most ancient breeds, probably descended from the extinct Turkmene horse and bred by the Turkoman tribes. Turkmenistan is an arid desert region surrounded by mountains: these rough conditions have produced a horse with incredible stamina, able to withstand great extremes of temperature, used to being tethered and fed a mixture of barley and alfalfa. One of the best recorded examples of the breed's endurance was in 1935, when a group of Akhal-Tekes traveled 2,500 miles from Ashkhabad to Moscow, in just 84 days. Domesticated for centuries, no one is quite sure if the Akhal-Teke is an example of a totally purebred breed or a descendant of the Turkoman horse from Iran. The Akhal-Teke itself has influenced a great many breeds including the Trakehner.

Description: Extremely elegant, with large intelligent eyes, long ears, as well as good legs and feet, chestnut is the most common color. (It is noted for having an almost metallic sheen to its coat.) The Akhal-Teke appears rather delicate, but this appearance is

AKHAL TEKE

deceptive, as this is a hardy breed. It has a fine-boned head, long neck, and long, straight back. Its legs are long and slim, although well-muscled and strong. Height stands at 15 to 15.2 hands (5ft to 5ft 1in).

BASHKIR

Origins: The Bashkir breed has been a feature of the mountains and steppes of the Urals for centuries, where it is bred primarily as a draft horse, but also as a source of milk or even meat when necessary. A number of horses conforming to this breed can also be found in the United States, where they are known as Bashkir Curlies. Some controversy has arisen over their origin, although they were first sighted in Nevada during the late 1890s. Unlike their Russian relatives, the American Bashkir Curlies are generally used as show horses or for long-distance and all-terrain competition riding. The Bashkir is sometimes crossed with

riding horses. Such breeds include the Don and imported Trotters.

Description: Hardy due to the extremely cold climate of the region, the Bashkir is short and stocky, with a layer of insulating fat and an adaptable coat. Short in summer, the coat becomes thick and curly during the winter months. This rich, coat, together with the Bashkirs' thick mane and coat are also frequently spun and woven into clothing. The Bashkir head is heavy, on a short, muscular neck. The back is comparatively long, and often hollow. Legs are short and sturdy, and the feet are rather small. Color is generally roan, chestnut, or bay, although there are variations. Height stands at around 14 hands (4ft 8in).

BUDYONNY/BUDENNY

Origins: A relatively new breed, the Budyonny gets its name from Marshall Budyonny, a hero of the Russian

Revolution. His aim was to develop a strong, skilful, intelligent, and adaptable breed for use as a military horse. This determination to create new, superior breeds was quite common in post-Revolution Russia of the 1920s. The breed was primarily developed at the military stud in Rostov, and the original crosses involved Don mares with English Thoroughbred stallions. Although experiments were made with other crosses, including Kazakh and Kirghiz, the Don-Thoroughbred cross proved the most successful. The breed was officially recognized in 1948, and its uses today have spread far beyond the original cavalry purpose. Its speed, stamina, and intelligence make it an ideal eventing and competition horse, including racing; both short and long distance and show-jumping.

Description: The Budyenny is a well-proportioned horse, with a medium head on a long neck. It has a long, straight back and sloping shoulders. Legs are long and slim, although powerful. Coat color is usually chestnut, although darker colors can occur. Height generally stands around 16 hands (5ft 4in).

DELIBOZ

Origins: The Deliboz was once considered to be a variation of the Kazakh breed that was also commonly found in the same areas of Azerbaijan. It was not until the 1940s that research showed the Deliboz to be a distinct and separate breed. Following the founding of the State Breeding Co-operative in 1943, formed with the purpose of preserving and fostering native horse breeds, the Deliboz bloodline was improved by crossing mares with Arabian and Kazakh stallions, and later by the introduction of Tersk blood.

Description: Primarily used as a saddle horse, the Deliboz is a hardy, sturdy horse, capable of traveling long distances while carrying heavy weights. It has a short head with a wide forehead, a sturdy, well-muscled neck, and a long back. It has well-formed legs that are sturdy and quite broad. Height stands at around 15 hands (5ft), and colors can vary from dark to light brown shades. A disadvantage of the Deliboz is that it has a somewhat nervous and unstable disposition.

DON

Origins: The original Don underwent some development during the 18th century with the introduction of Karabair and Karabakh blood. This was followed by cross-breeding with the Orlov at the beginning of the 19th century, and with the English Thoroughbred towards the end of the century. The Don is best known as the warhorse of the Cossack cavalry, renowned for its hardy constitution that enables it to live out the harsh Russian winters. This stamina contributed to the resilience of the Russian cavalry in pursuing Napoleon's troops in their retreat from Russia: the Don was able to survive where the French

horses could not. It is bred in the area around the Don and Volga Rivers. Major influences in the breed's development have been the Akhal-Teke, Arabian, and Thoroughbred.

Description: The modern Don is often used in long-distance endurance riding. Usual colors are chestnut and bay. The build of the Don is well-proportioned, and the horse has a long straight back and deep chest. Its legs are long, slim, and muscular. Height is between 15.3 and 16.2 hands (5ft 1in and 5ft 5in).

Estonian Native

Origins: Native bred for more than 900 years in Estonia, the Estonian Native is one of the world's most ancient breeds and there has been little crossing with other breeds, so the it retains many of its original characteristics. The Estonian has formed the basis of several modern breeds, including the Tori, produced by a cross with the Hackney breed, and the Estonian Draft, formed from a cross with the

Ardennes bloodline. As transportation and communication improved during the 15th century, the Estonian horse also became popular in Russia due to its strength and endurance, as well as its intelligence and ability to adapt to many kinds of work. It was during this period of increased demand for good working horses that breeding programs were introduced — both in terms of cross-breeding to create new breeds, and pure breeding. Eventually, however, the new breeds that had in many cases been partially founded on the Estonian, began to eclipse it as a work horse, and today it is little used in its native Estonia. However, a few are used in light farm work, although its primary use is in the burgeoning tourist trade, or as a riding horse for children. It does continue to be used as breeding stock, particularly for producing pony crosses.

Description: Bay, chestnut, and gray are most common colors for the Estonian Native, and height stands at around 14 hands (4ft 8in).

ESTONIAN

IOMUD

KABARDIN

IOMUD

Origins: Also known as the Iomudskaya (Russia) and Yamud (Iran). The Iomud is an ancient breed, sharing Turkoman origins with the Akhal-Teke from the same region of Turkmenistan. Bred and raised in the arid desert regions, the Iomud is exceptionally hardy, and able to live in the intense heat and harsh conditions without water for extended periods. Used for centuries as a general riding horse, as well as a cavalry horse, it also excels at competition riding, particularly cross country, where its skill in jumping, together with its stamina really come into their own.

Description: Arab blood is believed to have been introduced during the 14th century, and this influence can be seen in the Iomud's size: it is smaller and more compact than its Akhal-Teke relative. The Iomud has exceptionally strong legs and hard feet, necessary to cope with the rough terrain of its native land. It has a fine head on a sturdy neck, a long back, and a deep chest. It has well muscled, long legs. The coat color of the Iomud is generally gray, chestnut, or bay. Average height stands at around 14.2 to 15 hands (4ft 9in to 5ft).

KABARDIN

Origins: The origins of the Kabardin lie with the Arab and the now extinct Turkmene. These ancestors can be clearly seen in the Kabardin's appearance today. This breed is to be found in the steep and rocky Caucasus region, and is especially noted for being sure-footed and hardy. Often used as pack horses as well as riding horses, the breed was founded when tribesmen crossed Mongol stock with Persian blood. The breed was upgraded in the 20th century when Thoroughbred blood was introduced. This has resulted in a faster and taller horse: the Anglo-Kabardin. Today, the Kabardin is often exported and used as a sports horse, where it excels due to its natural speed and agility.

Description: It has an even temper, which, coupled with its intelligence, make it easy to train and quick to learn. The Kabardin has a light head on a long neck and a short back. It has a broad, deep chest and well-formed, muscular legs. Bay is the most common color, and height stands at 14.2 to 15.2 hands (4ft 9in to 5ft 1in).

KARABAIR

Origins: An ancient breed of Uzbekistan, the Karabair's origins are believed to be based on crosses between native mountain horses and Arabians. The Karabair has adapted well to its harsh mountain environment, and is intelligent, hardy and nimble. Its proportions and qualities have also seen the Karabair used in developing other breeds, particularly the Don. There are three main types of Karabair bred today. Although of equal size, their uses, and therefore their qualities are quite different. There is a heavy variety, which is the strongest and used for draft and harness work. The lighter variety is used as a riding or pack horse while the third type is a combination of the two. It is suitable both as a saddle horse, and for light draft work.

Description: The Karabair has a relatively small head, a long, muscular neck and a straight back. It has a deep chest, and well-proportioned, strong, stocky legs. Karabair coat coloration can be any solid color, although gray, chestnut, and black are common. Average Karabair height stands at about 14.2 to 15 hands (4ft 9in to 5ft).

KARABAKH

Origins: Another ancient breed of probably Oriental origins, this is a beautiful breed from the Caucasian region; it shares the metallic coat of the Akhal-Teke and is very similar to the Arab in conformation. It has previously been crossed with the Persian, Kabardin and Akhal-Teke. Native to a harsh and mountainous terrain, it is noted for being extremely agile and sure-footed and is used in the mounted games that are held in the region. Economical to keep and with a kindly nature, the Karabakh was used to further develop the Don horse, the famous mount of the Cossacks.

Description: The Karabakh has a small head set on a long neck, with a long, straight back. It has long slim legs, which are well muscled and powerful. The usual colors are dun or chestnut. Height stands at 14.2 hands (4ft 9in).

KUSHUM

Origins: Development of the Kushum began in the 1930s. Primarily, the aim was to produce a horse for use as a meat source, although once developed, the strong and energetic Kushum also proved a good solid military horse. The breeding program took place in the Kazakhstan region, and principal bloodlines utilized included Kazakh, Thoroughbred, and Don. Today the Kushum is a large horse, both in terms of height and weight. Its ready adaptability to different environments makes it an ideal

KARABAIR

work horse, while its easy annual weight gain means that meat production is high.

Description: The Kushum is characterized by its stocky, muscular appearance; a large head on a wide neck, broad chest, and strong withers. It has a long, straight back, a deep chest, and well-muscled, well-proportioned legs. The average height of a Kushum stallion stands at around 15.2 hands (5ft 1in), while the mare stands about 15 hands (5ft). Common coat colors are chestnut and bay.

KUSTANAIR

Origins: Based on an ancient Oriental horse breed, the Kustanair was developed in Kazakhstan during the 19th century. A selective breeding program first crossed Kazakh mares with Don and Orlov stallions, and later introduced English Thoroughbred blood. These crosses have led to two distinct types of Kustanair. The saddle horse is the lighter and more graceful of the two, sharing many of the characteristics of its Thoroughbred forebears. The light draft horse is stronger, more solid, and more readily adaptable to the harsh steppe environment. A third type also occurs, which contains characteristics of both main types, and which is suitable for either type of work.

Description: The Kustanair's characteristics include extremely strong legs and hooves and a strong musculature. It has a relatively small head on a muscular neck, a long back, and a broad, deep chest. It is an agile horse, which can move with surprising speed for its size, and also displays considerable endurance and stamina. Coat color is

LATVIAN

generally chestnut or bay, although other solid colors do occur. Height stands at around 15.1 hands (5ft).

LATVIAN

Origins: Like other continental draft breeds, the Latvian's ancestry is believed to derive from ancient heavy draft horses, native to northern Europe. Over the centuries, the various breeds have been lightened by cross-breeding, although until the 20th century the Latvian was still considerably heavier than today. The breed as we know it was officially recognized in the early 1950s. There are three main types of the Latvian breed. The heavy horse, also known as the Latvian Draft, was developed by introducing blood from standard draft horses, such as the Swedish and the Oldenburg. This strong, tough, and hard-working horse is the most common type of Latvian, and is used for transportation as well as draft work. The lighter version is used as a riding horse, both sport and pleasure, and

was produced through crosses with both Arab and Thoroughbred horses. It is the most recently developed of the three. The third type falls between these two in terms of strength, size, and weight. Also known as the Latvian Harness Horse, it has received blood from breeds such as the Hanoverian and Oldenburg, to produce a horse suitable for harness work, as well as competition riding.

Description: Characteristics include a long neck and short, muscular legs. Coat colors include chestnut, brown, and bay and height stands between 15.1 and 16 hands (5ft and 5ft 4in).

LITHUANIAN HEAVY DRAFT

Origins: Development of the Lithuanian Heavy Draft began towards the end of the 19th century, due to increasing demand for a locally-bred heavy draft horse for agricultural work. Native mares were crossed with Scandinavian breeds, including the Swedish Ardennes, and the result was

147

an extremely strong, well-muscled and well-proportioned horse, yet one which was of a medium size. The breed as we know it today was officially recognized in 1963. Still primarily used in agriculture today, the Lithuanian is also a useful meat source when food is scarce. It has also successfully been crossed with the Altai breed, to improve the Altai bloodline.

Description: The Lithuanian Heavy Draft is a tough horse, capable of coping with harsh environments. Characteristics include a heavy head, and particularly large feet. It is similar in appearance to the Latvian horse, and indeed shares much of the Latvian's ancestry. The head is medium-sized, with a particularly heavy jaw. The neck is broad, well muscled, and slightly arched. The legs are short

and muscular, particularly around the thighs. Color is generally chestnut and height is around 15.2 hands (5ft 1in).

LOKAI

Origins: The Lokai can be traced back to a breed of desert ponies kept by local tribes. Over the centuries the breed has been strengthened and improved by cross-breeding with Iomud, Karabair, Akhal-Teke, and Arab horses. The Lokai today is an attractive animal, ideally suited both as a pack and riding animal in its native land, and as a competition horse elsewhere. Today's animal is hardy, tough, and strong, possessing great stamina. These qualities, together with its nimbleness, means it is well able to survive and thrive in its harsh mountain environment. These same

LOKAI: TAJIKISTAN

qualities also make it sought after for sporting events.

Description: Of all the breeds that originated in Central Asia, the Lokai is the shortest. Although relatively small in stature, the Lokai is well-proportioned, and more generally classified as a small horse than as a pony. It is an adaptable and intelligent horse, and whether in the mountains or during sports events it displays considerable agility and endurance. The Lokai has a well-proportioned build, with a long neck, short back, and well-defined legs and feet. Most common coat colors are chestnut, bay, and gray, and the Lokai generally stands at around 14.3 hands (4ft 9in).

MÉTIS TROTTER

Origins: Also known as Russian Trotter. Until the beginning of the 20th century, the Russian Orlov Trotter was accepted as being the best racing trotter in the world. At around this time, however, the American Trotter more commonly known as the Standardbred began to overtake the Orlov. Determined to create a new, faster horse, Russian breeders imported American Standardbred horses with their own Orlovs. The result was the Métis Trotter, officially recognized in 1949.The breed has not yet beaten the American trotting horses, but it is faster than its Orlov relatives. The Métis Trotter is bred almost exclusively as a racing horse.

Description: It has a small head, long back and a broad chest, but the Métis Trotter's most distinctive characteristic must be its legs, which are often somewhat knock-kneed, giving the horse a rather peculiar stepping action. This defect is commonly known as "dishing." As well as being fast and energetic, the Métis Trotter has good stamina and possesses an equable temperament. A well-proportioned head is set on a long and muscular neck; the back is long and straight, the chest deep, and the legs well-formed and muscular. Common coat colors include chestnut, black, and gray, although any solid color is acceptable. Average height stands at around 15 to 15.3 hands (5ft to 5ft 1in).

NOVOKIRGHIZ

Origins: Also known as the New Kirgiz. The origins of the Novokirghiz lie with the hardy, native ponies of the nomadic tribesmen in the mountainous Kirghiz region. During the 1930s, a breeding program was established, crossing Old Kirghiz mares with Don and Thoroughbred stallions. The result is a small, tough, and strong riding horse, with many characteristics, such as excellent stamina and hardiness, of its mountain pony forebears. The Novokirghiz is a versatile horse, and is widely used as both a pack and riding horse and as a competition horse, where it excels at long-distance and cross-country racing. Its considerable strength, despite its small size, also makes it suitable for light draft work. The Novokirghiz also produces a good milk yield, and its milk is used to make the traditional drink of Kirghiz kumiss.

Description: The Novokirghiz has a sturdy and well-muscled body, with short legs and hard feet, necessary for coping with the rough terrain of its native region. Three distinct types can be found within the breed. These are the lighter saddle horse, the heavier massive horse, used for draft work, and the standard type, which combines elements of both other types. Novokirghiz coat color is generally brown, chestnut, or bay, and height stands between 14 and 15 hands (4ft 8in and 5ft).

ORLOV TROTTER

Origins: The Orlov was founded by Count Alexis Grigorievich Orlov, a Russian nobleman and Commander of the Russian fleet, who may have been involved with the murder of Czar Peter III. Orlov began by importing an Arabian stallion and putting it to a Danish mare. This resulted in a stallion named "Polkan;" he in turn fathered "Bars First." These animals formed the basis of the Orlov Trotter. The next step was the introduction of English, Arabian, Dutch, and Danish blood. The Orlov became the world's best trotting horse. Originally intended as a racehorse, the Orlov Trotter is also used for general harness work. Today, the development of the French Trotter and American Standardbred has rather eclipsed the Orlov. However, the Orlov has also made considerable contributions to the development of other breeds, including the Don.

Description: The Orlov is a handsome horse; the best have an Arab-like head, are tall, and lightly built. The head is medium in size, with a broad forehead. This is set on a long, well-muscled neck. The back is long, the chest deep, and the legs stocky, powerful, and solid. Quarters are strong. Height stands at around 16 hands (5ft 4in) but larger animals are known. The usual color is gray.

RUSSIAN HEAVY DRAFT

Origins: As agricultural needs changed during the 19th century, various Russian states began breeding programs to produce a smaller, lighter draft horse for use in agriculture. Selective breeding in the Ukraine, using native mares crossed with heavy draft breeds such as the Belgian, Percheron, and Swedish Ardennes, together with infusions of Orlov Trotter

blood, proved most successful. The Russian Heavy Draft breed gained widespread recognition during the Paris Exhibition of 1900, and its international success seemed assured. However, the upheavals caused by both the First World War and the Civil War, saw the breed almost destroyed, and it was not until the late 1930s that breeding could begin again.

Description: Now bred throughout the Soviet Union, the Russian Heavy Draft is extremely powerful, and well-muscled, although it is not of excessively large build. It is stocky, with a deep chest, short but well-muscled legs and hard hooves. The most common color is chestnut. Good-natured, fast for its size, and energetic, the average height stands between 14.1 and 15 hands (4ft 8in and 5ft).

SOVIET HEAVY DRAFT

Origins: The Soviet Heavy Draft is a relatively new arrival, being developed during the late 19th and early 20th centuries. Breed recognition came in 1952. The breed was developed using native mares and Belgian and Percheron stallions, and was intended to meet increasing demand for huge powerful horses for agricultural work, as farm production was escalating rapidly.

Description: A truly "heavy" horse, the Soviet Heavy Draft's relative speed belies its huge frame. It has a broad, powerful build, with well-muscled chest, legs, and neck. The neck is quite short, as are the legs, and the feet are particularly broad and solid. The Soviet Heavy Draft is a good all-round work horse, readily adaptable to a variety of tasks, and generally good natured and quick to learn. Believed to be the most popular heavy draft horse throughout the Soviet Union, the breed's gentle nature and stamina help account for its popularity. The Soviet Heavy Draft also provides a good source of milk and meat should circumstances require it. Color is usually bay or chestnut, and the average height of the breed stands at around 15.1 to 15.2 hands (5ft to 5ft 1in).

TERSKY

Origins: Also known as Tersk or Terek. Although a type of Tersky has existed for nearly 200 years, the modern-day Tersky was developed during the early years of the 20th century. Based on a type of Arabian Arab known as the Strelets, now extinct, the Tersky was created using English Thoroughbred, Kabardin, and Don blood. These bloodlines were introduced by Marshall Budyenny, and the Tersky was, and is, bred at two state studs Stavropol and Tersk, from which the breed gets its name. The original purpose of the breed was as a military horse, although as the years passed it became an important sporting breed, and this is its primary use today. The Tersky is an excellent show-jumper

SOVIET HEAVY DRAFT

and dressage horse, and possesses enough stamina to help it perform well in endurance riding.

Description: As well as these sporting attributes, the Tersky is also rightly famed for its particularly attractive appearance, and this beauty has made it a popular sight in both exhibitions and circuses. The Tersky is a gentle and graceful animal, and its good nature means that it is easy to train. Its Arab ancestry can be easily seen in both its appearance and bearing, and like the Arab, the Tersky has fine, well-formed features. The predominant Tersky color is an almost silvery gray, although bay and chestnut also occur. Height stands at between 14.3 and 15 hands (4ft 9in and 5ft).

Toric

Origins: The Toric was developed in the 19th century in Estonia, by crossing native Klepper draft horses with a variety of imported breeds, such as the Arab, English Thoroughbred, and Orlov Trotter. At the beginning of the 20th century, new blood infusions took place including Hanoverian and East Friesian. This selective breeding program produced the Toric we recognize today — an attractive, hard-working, and strong light draft horse. The Toric breed was not officially recognized until 1950, although it had already become a popular draft and agricultural horse by this time. Its particular pattern of cross-breeding means that the Toric is somewhat smaller than other draft breeds, although it has lost nothing in terms of power and strength. However, like several other draft breeds, there are two recognized types of Toric. The heavy type is generally used for the traditional draft work, while the lighter type is more often found working as a riding horse.

Description: A docile animal, the Toric adapts well to different types of work, has excellent stamina and is easy to train. The Toric's principal characteristics include short legs, a deep chest, and a larger than average head. The most usual coat colors of the Toric are bay and chestnut. Average height stands between 15 and 15.2 hands (5ft and 5ft 1in).

Ukrainian Riding Horse

Origins: Shortly after World War II, a breeding program began in Ukrainian studs for the purpose of creating a superior riding and sport horse. This selective process involved the crossing of mares from the Furioso, Nonius, and Gidran breeds, with Hanoverian, English Thoroughbred, and Trakehner stallions. Once the most suitable breeding combination was found, further infusions of Hanoverian and Thoroughbred were made, and the breed that became known as the Ukrainian Riding Horse was formed. The Ukrainian Riding Horse is indeed a high-class sporting and eventing animal, sharing the many excellent traits of its forebears. Colts are trained from an early age, and according to their particular talents they work in a wide range of disciplines, including show jumping, dressage, and racing (including cross-country). Horses that exhibit particular excellence at one or more disciplines are often retained for future breeding. Ukrainian Riding Horses have frequently performed extremely well at international competition level including the Olympics.

Description: The Ukrainian Riding Horse is large in stature, often with a large head. Its limbs and body are solid and well-muscled and its neck is long. It possesses considerable patience and stamina and may also be found working as a light draft horse as

well as in the sporting arena. Coat color is usually bay or chestnut. Height is around 16.1 hands (5ft 4in).

Vladimir

Origins: Heavy draft development of a new draft breed began towards the end of the 19th century, and continued until the Vladimir Heavy Draft breed gained formal recognition in 1946. Initial cross-breeding took place using local horses, and various common heavy draft breeds. These included the Percheron, Ardennais, and Clydesdale, and, for a limited period, the English Shire Horse. The intention of the breeders was to produce a powerful draft horse, that possessed more agility and speed than the draft breeds common at the time, which could often be rather lumbering. The Vladimir Heavy Draft is versatile, and suitable for all types of draft work. It is often used as a farm horse, and can also be used as a means of transport.

Description: The Vladimir Heavy Draft is a powerfully built draft horse, with a massive, well-muscled body, large head, strong neck, and short, thick legs. It has a graceful bearing for its large size, and is a rather attractive animal. It is capable of reaching, and maintaining, a reasonable speed, and it has a smooth pace. The Vladimir Heavy Draft has an even temper and a docile nature. Coat coloration is generally brown, chestnut, or black, and height stands between 15.2 and 16 hands (5ft 1in and 5 ft 4in).

Zhemaichu

Origins: Also known as Zhmud/Zhmudka. The modern day Zhemaichu is based on the smaller, native Lithuanian horses and ponies that have been found in the region for over 400 years. Since being domesticated, these horses have been used for farm work and as riding horses, and retain their usage in these ways to this day. Today's larger Zhemaichu came about due to selective breeding during the years after World War II. Stallions from draft breeds, primarily Swedish, were crossed with local mares. At each breeding the largest animals were used, until today's medium-built breed was produced. This breed is extremely adaptable and can perform well at a wide range of tasks, including both farm work as well as competition riding.

Description: The Zhemaichu has good stamina and strength, and can maintain speeds for considerable distances. It is a hardy animal, due to its long history in the often harsh conditions of its native region. The Zhemaichu is well-muscled and sturdy, and possesses a reasonably docile temperament. Coat coloration is generally bay, brown, or black. Height can stand up to 15.2 hands (5ft 1in), although smaller types can still be found, and these can reach an average of 13 hands (4ft 4in).

Lesser Known Breeds

AFRICA

DJERMA

Origins: Traditionally used by nomadic tribesmen, the Djerma can be found in western Africa, primarily in the middle part of the Niger region. It was developed using the Dongola and Barb breeds, and is a light, sturdy horse of average height. It is a hardy animal, being able to survive in extremely hot, dry conditions and has excellent endurance, traveling long distances without tiring.

Description: The Djerma is of stocky build, with well-muscled legs and a somewhat thick neck. Its coat is rough, and colors are usually dark tones such as dark brown or black. It stands at around 14 hands (4ft 8in).

DONGOLA

Origins: Also known as Dongalawi The Dongola is a rare breed, probably developed from early Barb horses. It can be found in northeast Africa, primarily in parts of Sudan and Eritrea. Its build is typical of horses located in harsh environments in that it is stocky and rather coarse in appearance. It is capable of enduring extremes of heat and aridity, and can survive on sparse amounts of food and water.

Description: The Dongola's coat is usually bay with a reddish tint and it stands around 14 hands (4ft 8in). The Dongola has been used in the development of such local breeds as the Sudanese Country Bred, as well as the Djerma.

FLEUVE

Origins: Named by the French colonists as the Cheval de Fleuve, or River Horse, due to its proximity to local rivers, the Fleuve originated in western Africa, and is principally found in Senegal.

Description: A light horse breed, it was developed by cross-breeding Barb horses with indiginous pony stock. The result is a stocky, hardy breed, well able to cope in Africa's climate. At 14 to 14.3 hands (4ft 8in to 4ft 9in) in height, the Fleuve is usually brown.

FRANCE

LIMOUSIN HALFBRED

Origins: The original Limousin was an old breed favored during the Middle Ages as a warhorse. Its origins were primarily Barb. However, over the centuries, the breed was regularly crossed with both the Arab and the Arab-based English Thoroughbred.

Description: Its appearance today is considerably different from the original horse. Similar to a pure Arab, it is not quite as finely built and is somewhat taller. Stong and intelligent, the Limousin Halfbred is usually bay or chestnut in color and generally stands between 15 to 16 hands (5ft to 5ft 4in).

JAPAN

BAN-EI

Origins: The Ban-ei is a heavy draft breed with a rather unusual use.

Although some horses of the breed can be found doing traditional draft or agricultural work, the Ban-ei is primarily bred as a race horse. However, the race it performs in is a special race known as the Ban-ei-Keiba, and requires the horse to pull a heavy sledge, necessitating its bulk and strength. The main breeds used in development of the Ban-ei were the French heavy draft breeds, the Breton and Percheron.

Description: The Ban-ei exhibits all the characteristics of its forebears in terms of power and size, but also possesses speed and agility. Coat color can be any solid color, and the Ban-ei stands anywhere between 14.3 and 16.1 hands (4ft 9in and 5ft 4in).

TAISHUH

Origins: The Taishuh is an ancient breed, tracing its origins back to the original Asiatic horses and poines. The current breed is believed to have developed in the 8th century. It is a very rare breed, with less than 100 believed to survive today.

Description: Strong, stocky, and sturdy, the Taishuh is hardy and adaptable to harsh conditions. It is a gentle animal, ideally suited as a children's or beginner's riding horse. Originally classified as a pony breed, it is today considered that the Taishuh may well exhibit more horse characteristics.

PAKISTAN

BALUCHI

Origins: Found in various regions of northern Pakistan, such as Baluchistan, Bahawalpur, and Multan, the Baluchi horse is a strong, stocky horse, bearing some resemblence to the ancient Asiatic horses and ponies.

It is likely that cross-breeding with imported breeds has occured over the years, although the precise origins of the Baluchi are not known. The Baluchi is used as a riding horse and to pull the native wagons.

Description: Hardy and powerful for their size, with good stamina, Baluchi are well-formed in appearance with a light head on a long neck. Legs are slim but well muscled. The Baluchi is usually chestnut or bay, and stands at around 14.2 hands (4ft 9in).

USA

NORTH AMERICAN SINGLE-FOOTING HORSE

Origins: The primary qualities required in the Single-Footing Horse are all to do with pace. It has been developed specifically to excel at all kinds of trail riding, whether this be riding for pleasure, working, such as ranching, or sport riding, including long-distnace and cross-country. To meet the required standards, a Single-Footing Horse must have a smooth, comfortable gait that it must be able to maintain for long distances and at reasonable speeds. It is this gait that gives rise to the name "Single-Footer."

Description: An attractive horse of light build, the Single-Footer is also hardy, intelligent, and possesses great stamina. It has an even temper, and is generally quick and willing to learn. There is no size or color restriction for a Single-Footing Horse. A well-proportioned build is essential, but it is the gait that is of primary importance.

ARAAPPALOOSA

Origins: Although only recently registered in the US, the Arappaloosa is not a new horse type. It was first developed in the 1930s by Claude Thompson who had long admired the Appaloosa breed, one of the oldest in America, and felt that an infusion of Arab blood would create an even more beautiful horse.

Description: The result is an extremely high-quality horse, exhibiting all the finest qualities of the founding Appaloosa breed in terms of markings, performance, temperament, and stamina, as well as the refinements introduced by the Arab blood — enhanced color, lightness of build, and elegance.

GOLDEN AMERICAN SADDLEBRED

Origins: A fusion of the American Saddlebred and Palomino breeds, the Golden American Saddlebred is a particularly beautiful horse. The first horse recognized as a Golden American Saddlebred was born in 1864, although the breed was not recognized by the Palomino registry until 75 years later.

Description: Extremely well-proportioned. A Golden Amrican Saddlebred has a long, arched neck, short back, and slim, well-muscled legs. It has an elegant bearing and is strong, intelligent ,and adaptable. The breed is often found in shows or exhibitions, and it has the perfect temperament for performance, being proud and somewhat high-spirited. Golden American Saddlebreds are also used as traditional riding horses. Coat color must be a clean shade, and can be various hues from cream to gold to copper. The horse stands between 15 and 17 hands (5ft and 5ft 8in).

MOYLE

Origins: A very rare breed, developed by Rex Moyle during the 1940s-1950s. His intention was to create a light riding horse, suitable primarily for trail work. His base stock was the common Mustang, brought from Utah to Idaho, where he had his ranch.

Description: The Moyle riding horse eventually developed into a lightly built horse with the stocky build and hardiness of the Mustang, and an even temperament. Suitable for all types of riding, from pleasure to long distance, the Moyle is little known, and centred around one area. The Moyle is of average height, and generally brown.

QUARAB

Origins: A recently-registered breed, the Quarab, as its name would suggest, is a cross between the Quarter Horse and Arab breeds. Formally recognized in 1989, the breed was extended in 1991 to include Paint Horses, with their distinctive markings. Registration into the breed is very strict. Both sire and dam must be registered with one of the three breeds.

Description: Quarab build can either follow its fine-boned and elegant Arab relatives, or the somewhat stockier frame of the Quarter Horse. The head

ALTAI

156

is generally light, the neck arched, and the legs slim but muscular. The Quarab has been found to excel at a variety of disciplines, including competition events such as dressage, driving, and riding. Color and markings vary, and the Quarab stands between 14 to 16 hands (4ft 8in to 5ft 4in).

THE FORMER USSR

ALTAI

Origins: Developed over a long period of time in the harsh mountain regions of parts of the former Soviet Union.

Description: The Altai is a stocky, rather coarse horse, with short, solid, and well-muscled legs. It exhibits excellent stamina and hardiness, necessary to endure the harsh conditions of its native regions. The Altai is of average height, with stallions standing at, and mares just under 14 hands (4ft 8in). Coat coloration is generally bay, black, and chestnut, and some markings such as spots can be found. The Altai has been crossed with several breeds such as the Russian and Soviet Heavy Drafts to produce a larger and stronger horse, and these cross-breeds are often used as meat sources.

ANGLO-KABARDA

Origins: Developed during the 1930s at two Caucasian studs, the Anglo-Karbarda is a cross between Kabardin mares and English Thoroughbred stallions. The Thoroughbred blood is usually dominant, and the Anglo-Kabarda is most like the Thoroughbred in appearance and conformation.

157

Description: A hardy horse, the Anglo-Kabarda is well-suited to survival in the harsh climate and rocky terrain of the Caucasus. They are also used outside their native region, finding success as riding horses and also at sporting events. In fact, the Anglo-Kabarda frequently participates in many horse events and is successful at an international level, including the Olympics.

BYELORUSSIAN HARNESS HORSE

Origins: Based on the ancient heavy horses native to the northern regions of eastern Europe, the Byelorussian Harness Horse was developed by introducing blood from breeds such as the Belgian Ardennes, though its principal progenitor is the Norwegian Dole. Two distinct types can be easily identified. One is heavier, while the other is of medium build and more suitable for light draft work.

Description: The Byelorussian Harness Horse is a hardy animal, extremely well-adapted to the rough country terrain of its native region. As well as farm work, the horse is also a good source of meat and milk for the local people. A muscular, well-formed animal, with a thick neck and solid legs, the Byelorussian horse is most commonly chestnut and bay. Height stands at around 15 to 15.3 hands (5ft to 5ft 2in).

BYELORUSSIAN